W 3   2210
Max   Maxwell, John
           Partners In Prayer

DATE DUE

DEMCO

PARTNERS IN PRAYER

John Maxwell

THOMAS NELSON PUBLISHERS
Nashville • Atlanta • London • Vancouver

Published in Nashville, Tennessee, by Thomas Nelson, Inc., and distributed in Canada by Word Communications, Ltd., Richmond, British Columbia, and in the United Kingdom by Word (UK), Ltd., Milton Keynes, England.

Unless otherwise noted Scripture quotations are taken from the HOLY BIBLE, NEW INTERNATIONAL VERSION ®. Copyright © 1973, 1978, 1984 by International Bible Society. Used by permission of Zondervan Bible Publishing House. All rights reserved.

The "NIV" and "New International Version" trademarks are registered in the United States Patent and Trademark Office by International Bible Society. Use of either trademark requires the permission of International Bible Society.

Scripture quotations noted NASB are taken from THE NEW AMERICAN STANDARD BIBLE ®, © Copyright The Lockman Foundation 1960, 1962, 1963, 1968, 1971, 1972, 1973, 1975, 1977. Used by permission.

Scripture quotations noted AMPLIFIED are from THE AMPLIFIED BIBLE: Old Testament. Copyright © 1962, 1964 by Zondervan Publishing House (used by permission); and from THE AMPLIFIED NEW TESTAMENT. Copyright © 1958 by the Lockman Foundation (used by permission).

Personal letters in chapters 6 and 8 are used by permission.

Library of Congress Cataloging-in-Publication Data
Maxwell, John C., 1947–
    Partners in prayer : how to revolutionize your church with a team prayer strategy / John C. Maxwell.
      p. cm.
    ISBN 0-7852-7439-1 (pbk.)
    1. Prayer—Christianity. 2. Church growth. I. Title.
BV210.2.M38 1996
248.3′2—dc20   96–8947
                                         CIP

Printed in the United States of America
6 7 - 02 01 00 99 98 97

DEDICATION

This book is dedicated to . . .

Bill Klassen,
more like Moses than any man I've ever met,
who started the prayer partner ministry
and who has prayed and stood in the gap for me
every day for the last fifteen years.

Fred Rowe,
Bill's and my Joshua,
who has become a great prayer warrior in his own right
and who continues to intercede for me and INJOY daily.

The 120 Prayer Partners at Skyline,
whose powerful and protective prayers are
responsible for any success I've known as a
husband, father, and church leader.

CONTENTS

Foreword by Max Lucado

About the Author

FOREWORD

BY MAX LUCADO

Some months ago I enjoyed a four-week summer sabbatical. I set three goals during the month. First, I wanted to plan an autumn series of lessons on grace (which I did). Second, I aspired to break ninety on the golf course (I did that too—once). And third, I wanted to learn more about leadership skills. It was through this third goal that I came to know John Maxwell.

A coworker recommended I seek his advise, so I gave him a call. He invited me to come and speak to the Skyline congregation in San Diego. I did. I gathered some ideas on leadership, but much more, I gained a passion for Prayer Partners.

My Sunday at Skyline was bathed in prayer. The Prayer Partners met me as I walked in the door and met me as I walked off the platform. They were praying for me as I flew, as I spoke, even as I rested. I was so convicted about the importance of Prayer Partners that I asked God to grant me 120 members who would covenant to pray for me daily and pray with me fervently.

Upon returning to the pulpit I announced my dream to the congregation. Within a month exactly 120 people had volunteered to form the team. We divided the volunteers into four groups and assigned each group one Sunday per month on which they would arrive early and pray for the congregation.

That was six months ago. Has God honored the prayers of his people? Here is a sample of what God has done since we organized Prayer Partners:

- We have broken our Sunday attendance record twice.
- We finished the year with our highest ever average Sunday attendance.

- We finished the year—hang on to your hat—*over* budget.
- We added three new staff members and six new elders.
- We witnessed several *significant* physical healings.
- I completed a challenging book on grace.
- Our entire staff attended a part of the inaugural Promise Keepers Pastors Conference.
- Our church antagonism is down, and church unity is high.

And most significantly, we called the church to forty days of prayer and fasting, inviting God to shine his face upon us. God has honored the prayers of His people. More than ever I'm convinced: When we work, we work; but when we pray, God works.

Thank you, John Maxwell, for your example. Thank you for going to the effort of putting into print what you have put into practice. I speak for thousands who will benefit from this book when I say: You're a friend to all who dream of a growing kingdom.

1

UNLEASHING THE POTENTIAL OF PRAYER

Show me your ways, O LORD, teach me your paths;
guide me in your truth and teach me, for you are
God my Savior, and my hope is in you all day long.
Psalm 25:4–5

I grew up in a Christian household where prayer was important. And as a pastor, I spent time in prayer every day. But it wasn't until God brought me a prayer partner that my life and ministry exploded with power, and the results began to multiply in an incredible way.

It all started in 1981 when I became the senior pastor at Skyline Wesleyan Church in San Diego, California. My wife, Margaret, and I moved to San Diego with our children, Elizabeth and Joel Porter, after I spent two years as the executive director of evangelism at Wesleyan World Headquarters in Indiana. Before that I had spent eleven years as the pastor of two churches in Indiana and Ohio.

I was excited about being a pastor again, and especially about coming to Skyline. I was eager to get to know the staff, evaluate the church's ministries, assess the leadership, and identify the key leaders who were going to help me accomplish the church's mission. I was trying to accomplish as much as I could as quickly as I could, which was making me maintain a very heavy schedule.

On a Tuesday morning after I'd been at Skyline for about six weeks, I was reviewing the day's schedule when I saw an appointment scheduled for a person whose name I didn't recognize.

"Who's Bill Klassen?" I asked.

"He's your ten o'clock appointment," replied Barbara, my assistant.

"I see that, but who is he? Is he in leadership?" I asked. I had spent the last few weeks focusing much of my attention on getting to know the leaders in the congregation.

"No, he's not in leadership," said Barbara. "As a matter of fact, he doesn't even go to church at Skyline." Barbara could see that I wasn't happy. "He said he had to see you. He was very persistent," she added emphatically.

"Well," I said, "give me about fifteen minutes with him, and if we're not done, interrupt us." My plan was to figure out what his agenda was, fix whatever problem he had, kindly but quickly, and get on with the work I had to get done that day.

ONE LAYPERSON CALLED TO PRAY

Bill turned out to be a gentleman of about sixty with hair white as snow. His face was gentle, almost radiant. He reminded me a little bit of Moses as he might have looked coming down from Mount Sinai. He began telling me about himself, how he had worked in construction in Canada and sold sailboats in Washington and southern California, and how he had worked for the Navigators ministry as a discipler.

"John," Bill said. "I believe God has called me—a layman—to disciple, encourage, and pray for pastors. And the reason I came here today was so that I could pray for you."

He wanted to pray for me? I thought. *In all my years as a pastor, I've never had a layman come just to pray for me.* My own agenda began to melt away. I felt the spirit of God crushing me, saying, "John, My agenda is more important than yours. Your life is not like a one-way street where you just minister to other people. There are people who want to minister to you. I am sending this layman to pray for you."

When Barbara came in to interrupt us, I sent her away. Bill and I spent probably an hour praying together that day, and I wept at the knowledge that God would send someone just to pray for me. Bill fulfilled a need for personal prayer that I didn't know I had, and he sparked a deep desire for an additional prayer covering over me, the church, my family, and my ministry.

A while later, Bill told me that he had been praying eighteen months for God to bring him a pastor to pray for. After our first meeting that day, he went home and immediately talked to Marianne, his wife.

"I found our pastor today, Marianne," he said. "I haven't heard him preach, but I've heard him pray." The following Sunday Bill and Marianne came to church and sat in a pew near the front. They've been sitting there ever since.

THE POWER OF PARTNERING IN PRAYER

Neither of our lives has ever been the same since that meeting. Bill became my personal prayer and accountability partner after that, and he went on to help me organize a prayer partner ministry at Skyline, a group of people who prayed for me every day during my fourteen years there and who met in small groups in a tiny room at church every Sunday to cover the services with prayer. It started with thirty-one laymen and eventually expanded to include 120.

During those fourteen years, the congregation tripled in size from a little over 1,000 to nearly 3,500. The church's annual income jumped from $750,000 to more than $5,000,000. Ministry at

Skyline flourished, with lay involvement increasing from 112 to over 1,800 people.

But the really awesome power of those prayers has been in individual lives: Thousands of people received Christ during those years. My prayer partners grew in their walk with God and became active participants in the miraculous power of prayer in their daily lives. Bill and Marianne Klassen started their own ministry to teach other churches how to start their own prayer partners. And during those years, God led me down an incredible road. In addition to all the wonderful things happening in the church, I began working more and more with other pastors, teaching them leadership and church growth. I formed INJOY, a nondenominational Christian organization dedicated to helping leaders reach their potential, in the church, business, and the family. I've even had the privilege of speaking at several Promise Keepers conferences around the country.

Without prayer and the power of the Holy Spirit, I believe none of these things would have happened. The glory and the honor belong to God. But the credit for releasing that power and keeping me protected day after day belongs to those prayer partners.

PRAYER PARTNERS IN HISTORY

Laypeople partnering in prayer with godly leaders is not a new concept. It goes all the way back to the Old Testament in the book of Exodus when Moses prayed on a hilltop for Joshua to defeat the Amalekites (I discuss the incident in greater detail in chapter 5). It continued in the New Testament, particularly in the first days of the developing first-century church, as recounted in the book of Acts. You probably remember how the 120 disciples prayed during the days between Jesus' ascension and the day of Pentecost (Acts 1:14). On the day when the Holy Spirit arrived, a simple fisherman named Peter gave his testimony, and 3,000 people were converted.

Over the centuries, there have undoubtedly been innumerable

instances of people partnering in prayer with preachers. Though no records exist outside of heaven for most of them, we do know the story of some fairly recent ones:

The Preacher: Charles Finney

The Year: 1830

The Place: Rochester, New York

The Results: In one year 1,000 of the city's 10,000 inhabitants came to Christ.

The Partner: Finney's "prayer partner" was Abel Clary. Finney wrote, "Mr. Clary continued as long as I did and did not leave until after I had left. He never appeared in public, but gave himself wholly to prayer."

The Preacher: D. L. Moody, an Obscure YMCA Worker

The Year: 1872

The Place: London, England

The Results: In ten days 400 new converts came into the church where he was preaching.

The Partner: In London, a bedridden girl, Marianne Adlard, had read a clipping about Moody's ministry in Chicago and prayed that God would send him to her church.

The Preacher: Canadian Missionary Jonathan Goforth

The Year: 1909

The Place: Manchuria, China

The Results: A great revival throughout Manchuria

The Partner: While in London later that year, Goforth was taken to see an invalid lady. As they talked about the revival in Manchuria, she asked him to look at her notebook. She had recorded three days when special power came upon her for his meetings in Manchuria. A feeling of awe gripped Goforth as he realized those were the very days he witnessed the greatest power in Manchuria.

The Preacher: Southern Revivalist Mordecai Ham

The Year: 1934

The Place: Charlotte, North Carolina

The Results: Many people in Charlotte were deeply moved, including a farmer's son named Billy Graham who was converted.

The Partners: Several businessmen, along with Billy Graham's father, had spent a day at the Graham farm praying that God would touch their city, their state, and their world.

The Preacher: Billy Graham

The Year: 1949

The Place: Los Angeles, California

The Results: An extended campaign that resulted in a change of approach in reaching people for Christ—leading to a new era of mass evangelism.

The Partners: Graham had conducted many similar events with much smaller results. He later realized that the only difference between the L.A. crusade and all the others before it had been the amount of prayer he and his people had given it.

These instances attest to the tremendous power of prayer partnerships. It doesn't matter whether the leader is a pastor or layman, and the person praying can be a man, woman, or child—when someone behind the scenes partners in prayer with one of God's frontline servants, awesome things happen.

PRAYER CHANGES THE WORLD

There's no telling how much the world has changed as the result of the silent prayers of Christians throughout history. Prayer is powerful! John Wesley recognized that power when he said:

> Give me 100 preachers who fear nothing but sin and desire nothing but God, and I care not a straw whether they be clergy or laymen, such alone will shake the gates of hell and set up the kingdom of Heaven on earth. God does nothing but in answer to prayer.

God's hand moves when people and pastors pray together. Through prayer, God makes the impossible, possible.

Through prayer, God greatly multiplies our efforts. C. H. Spurgeon said, "Whenever God determines to do a great work, He first sets His people to pray." In a moment of revelation, Spurgeon had discovered that neither his sermons nor his good works accounted for the spiritual impact of his ministry. Instead, it was, as one writer put it, "The prayers of an illiterate lay brother who sat on the pulpit steps pleading for the success of the sermons." It was his partnership with people of prayer that made him effective.

I can personally attest to the benefits that others' prayers have given me. There have been times when I've gotten ready to do a service or conference, and I've been physically exhausted. But when my prayer partners lay hands on me, and I see them praying over the auditorium, I receive a new strength—physically, mentally, spiritually, and emotionally. I feel prepared to receive the power of God. And that has allowed my ministry to have great impact on people's lives.

My prayer partners have also told me, "Pastor, during the service we are going to cover the people around us in prayer. When you see us in the service, we'll give you a thumbs-up. That way you'll know we're praying for you, and we have our area covered." When we've had a particularly good service, I know my partners and their prayers were the reason for it.

I will never forget the Church Growth conference INJOY held in Anderson, Indiana, a couple of years ago. About 2,500 people were in attendance, and several of my prayer partners were in the audience. I was onstage with Sheryl Fleisher, a fellow pastor and friend. While Sheryl was speaking, an administrative person from the university where we were holding the conference came hurriedly down the center aisle toward the stage. I could tell from her expression and body language that something was wrong.

"John," she said, "I just got word that a tornado touched down about two miles from here, and it's headed straight for us."

I interrupted Sheryl and calmly directed the people to take shelter in the basement. As everyone moved toward the stairs, Brad Hansen, our worship leader, came up on stage with his accompanist, Terry Hendricks, and they softly played and led us in "Nothing But the Blood of Jesus." About three-fourths of the group was able to squeeze into the basement, and the rest lined the walls. A few of us remained on stage while Brad continued to lead worship. As I looked around, I saw Bill Klassen and a few of the prayer partners praying, and I began to pray, too, commanding Satan and his forces to draw back by the power of God.

Within a few minutes, we got word that the tornado had suddenly turned north, and we were clear of any further threat. The teaching time was especially sweet that day after everyone returned to the auditorium. And more than 100 people committed to full-time Christian service at that conference. The prayers of those few faithful people put in motion the power of God, prevented an almost certain disaster, and helped to build God's kingdom.

PRAYER CHANGES ME

Jesus told His disciples, "I tell you the truth, my Father will give you whatever you ask in my name. Until now you have not asked for anything in my name. Ask and you will receive, and your joy will be complete" (John 16:23-24). If prayer did nothing other than what Jesus promised, it would be one of the greatest gifts God has given us. But prayer does even more. It changes the ordinary man or woman and makes them extraordinary.

Prayer changes us by drawing us closer to God, changing and molding us into His likeness in the process. David understood prayer's power as a personal change agent. His prayer in Psalm 25:4-5 describes the process that prayer takes a person through: "*Show me* your ways, O LORD, *teach me* your paths; *guide me* in your truth and teach me, for you are God my Savior, and my hope is in you all day long" (emphasis added).

This passage contains three key phrases: *show me, teach me,* and *guide me.* When God *shows us* His standards and His will for our lives, it isn't always easy on us. It almost always requires us to grow and change. But once we accept what God would show us, He is able to *teach us.* And when we're teachable and growing, He is finally able to *guide us,* to lead us into His plan and purpose. When God shows me, He has my heart. When God teaches me, He has my mind. When God guides me, He has my hand.

We grow to meet the challenges we pray for. I am reminded of the story of a climbing expedition to Mount Everest in 1924. A group of climbers tried twice to get to the top of the world's tallest mountain but failed. In fact, two of their party were killed in that endeavor. They met in London a few weeks later to talk about it and give a report before a crowd of interested supporters.

On the stage was a large picture of Mount Everest. One of the men stood up to speak. As he addressed the crowd, he turned to the picture of Mount Everest and said, "You have conquered us once, you have conquered us twice, but Mount Everest, you will not conquer us every time." He turned to the audience and with determination said, "Because Mount Everest can grow no larger, but we can."

DON'T LIVE BENEATH YOUR POTENTIAL

Despite God's promise of the power of prayer to change us and our world, many Christians never tap into it. They come to Christ, but then they live beneath their privileges. It's as though God has prepared an incredible banquet for them, and they're sitting in the corner with a bologna sandwich. The problem is that they don't want to risk giving up the familiar sandwich for the promise of the banquet. It's almost like they're saying, "Okay, I'm saved and I'm going to heaven, but I'm going to stay right where I am until then."

I must ask you: Are you one of those living beneath your privileges and missing out on your potential by not praying? The table has been laid. The sumptuous banquet has been set out. You have already received your invitation. Now what are you going to do? Are you going to bring along a few friends and come to the table? Or are you going to eat your bologna sandwich alone in a corner? The choice is yours. You *can* become a person of prayer who receives and shares the blessings God has to give.

Most pastors and their churches across the country are currently starving in the area of prayer. One evangelical pastor, speaking about his own denomination, said, "In Acts chapter two, they prayed for ten days. Peter preached for ten minutes and 3,000 were saved. Today, churches pray for ten minutes, preach for ten days and three get saved."

But it doesn't have to be that way. Every pastor at every church in this country can tap into the awesome power and protection that only prayer provides. I believe that you may be one of the people in your church who can help make that happen.

You may be saying to yourself, "Me? I'm no prayer warrior. I could never lead or organize others to pray. I'm not even comfortable with the idea of praying for my pastor. I don't even know if I can do it."

My answer is, "Yes you can!" Anyone can become a strong man or woman of prayer. It doesn't take a miracle, and you don't have to be a Holy Roller. You only need to be a Christian. If you meet that qualification, you have the potential to become a great pray-er. And that's the reason you can pray for your church leaders. You are on the same level as them in the eyes of God. A pastor is simply a brother in Christ, not some spiritual giant. He struggles with the same problems you do.

Get ready to go on an exciting journey, one that will help you, your pastors, and your church reach their potential. We'll start out slow, first talking about some of the fundamentals of prayer and how you can improve your personal prayer life. Then we'll broaden our focus to include how you can pray for others, including your pastors (or elders and other leaders) and church, showing how you can become a partner in prayer. And finally, we'll talk about the hope that we all have for our churches and our country—revival.

DISCUSSION QUESTIONS

1. What's the greatest "answered prayer" story you've ever heard?

2. Think of the examples of people who've prayed behind the scenes in history. Have there been events in your life where someone might have been praying behind the scenes for you?

3. How would you describe your current prayer life?
   a. eating a bologna sandwich
   b. checking out the menu
   c. sampling the hors d'oeuvres
   d. feasting at the banquet
   e. feasting and bringing others along with you to the banquet

4. Describe what could happen if a core group of people in your congregation prayed daily for the church and the pastor(s).

5. C. H. Spurgeon said, "Whenever God determines to do a great work, He first sets His people to pray." What great work is God currently desiring that you pray for?

2

GETTING TO KNOW YOUR FATHER

Come near to God and he will come near to you.
James 4:8

One night in 1968, the pilot of an airliner bound for New York realized that the landing gear of his jet would not engage. Traveling ever closer to his destination, he continued to work the controls, trying to get the wheels to lock into place, but he had no success. Circling over the airport, he asked the control tower for instructions. The ground crew, responding to the impending crisis, sprayed the runway with foam, and emergency vehicles moved into position. The pilot was instructed to land the plane as best he could.

The passengers were asked to prepare themselves for the worst and to put themselves into crash position. Moments before landing, the pilot announced over the intercom: "We are beginning our final descent. In accordance with International Aviation Codes established at Geneva, it is my obligation to inform you that if you believe in God, you should commence praying." The plane then performed a belly landing, and miraculously, came to a stop with no injury to the passengers.

If that pilot hadn't found himself in a crisis that day, his passengers would never have known about the airline's hidden provision for prayer. But isn't that the way it is for most people? As long as everything's going smoothly, they rarely think about talking to God. But as soon as a situation becomes life or death, they turn to Him for help.

That kind of thinking is almost to be expected among nonbelievers. Many of them have a "flat-tire mentality." As long as they're cruising down the highway of life and the car is handling the road well, then everything's great. But when there's a blowout, they turn to God.

WHY BELIEVERS DON'T PRAY

The remarkable thing is that many Christians spend as little time communicating with God as nonbelievers. Why is that? Have many lost their belief in the power of prayer? William A. Ward said, "God is never more than a prayer away from you. . . . We address and stamp a letter and send it on its way, confident that it will reach its destination, but we doubtfully wonder if our prayer will be heard by an ever-present God."

I think the main reason people don't spend much time praying is that they have the wrong attitude toward prayer. Some people think of prayer as something only their grandmother does. Or they think of the simple prayers of their childhood: "God is great. God is good. Let us thank Him for our food. Amen," or "Now I lay me down to sleep. . . ."

But even people who have a genuine desire to pray and have tried to develop a prayer life sometimes have the wrong idea about it. They think that in order to pray they have to go off by themselves, get on their knees, close their eyes, fold their hands, etc. They take with them a list of things to pray about, and then they go through the list methodically. None of those things are bad or wrong, but that kind of mechanical prayer life can become very tedious. For most people, after about five minutes they run out of things to say, become frustrated, and then feel guilty for not having a better prayer life. No wonder so many Christians are reluctant to pray. They've made prayer a formal, stiff, lifeless thing that it was never meant to be. Any time the mechanics of prayer get in the way of loving God, they're a hindrance, not a help.

TALKING TO A FRIEND

Prayer should be the most natural thing in the world, like speaking your mind with a friend you trust. C. Neil Strait said, "Prayer is . . . talking with God and telling him you love Him . . . conversing with God about all the things that are important in life, both large and small, and being assured that He is listening."

First and foremost, prayer is talking to your Father in heaven and getting to know Him. It's the process of developing a relationship. How do you develop and grow in your relationship with God? The same way you do with anyone else. You spend time together. Armand Nicholi of Harvard University Medical School said, "Time is like oxygen; there's a minimum amount that's necessary for survival. And it takes quantity, as well as quality, to develop warm and caring relationships."

IT'S A LITTLE LIKE A MARRIAGE

Think of your relationship with God as being similar to a marriage. The main difference is that God, unlike your spouse, is perfect. He loves you unconditionally, is absolutely trustworthy, and forgives you for *anything and everything* you do wrong—past, present, and future—if only you ask. The good news is that God has already done the hard work in the relationship. All we have to do is be willing to communicate with Him, and we can learn to do that.

Look at some of the married couples you know. You can see that in a good marriage the partners talk about everything. Their communication is spontaneous, transparent, and open. They don't hold anything back, and they don't try to manipulate each other. But when communication becomes stiff, formal, or nonexistent, marriages deteriorate. Studies indicate that half of all divorces result from bad communication.

Marriage expert Gary Smalley has said that a healthy marriage relationship requires one hour of communication a day. This ensures the continual development and deepening of the relationship. And I try to spend that amount of time with my wife, Margaret, every day. How do you think she would feel if the only time I communicated with her was in an emergency?

The same is true with God. A deep relationship with Him takes time and effort. It cannot be formed in just a few fleeting mechanical moments. And it can't be built on an emergency basis either. E. M. Bounds once wrote, "God's acquaintance is not made hurriedly. He does not bestow His gifts on the casual or hasty comer and goer. To be much alone with God is the secret of knowing Him and of influence with Him."

If we can change our attitudes toward prayer—thinking of it as a process that builds our relationship with God—and cultivate a daily prayer time, we can become strong people of prayer. And the prayer life we develop has the potential to completely transform our lives.

Before we get into some of the specifics of how to pray, let me give you five guidelines that will help you have the right attitude toward prayer:

1. Be Spontaneous

Try to put out of your mind once and for all that prayer has to be tedious or repetitive. Instead it should be spontaneous and exciting. That doesn't mean that prayer time will always be happy and fun. There will be times when you hurt and cry to God for consolation, other times when you shout at Him in anger. But you will also laugh and have a good time. The main thing is for you to be yourself.

What does it mean to maintain a spontaneous spirit? Let's say, for example, that you pray in the morning when you get up. On a particular morning as you look at your prayer list, you may feel agitated and distracted. Rather than trying to fight with that agitation and suppress it, talk to God about it first. And if you can't figure out what's bothering you, ask God to reveal it to you. Clearing the air as you begin to pray may be just what you need to do in order to better communicate with God. Or it may be something that God wants you to spend all of your time praying about on that particular day.

Willingness to share yourself with God is a matter of the heart and the attitude. We can close ourselves off, refusing to grow in our relationship, or we can be willing to tell God everything on our minds and hearts. Francois Fenelon expressed this idea well with the following words:

> Tell God all that is in your heart, as one unloads one's heart, its pleasures and its pains, to a dear friend. Tell Him your troubles, that He may comfort you; tell Him your joys, that He may sober them; tell Him your longings, that He may purify them; tell Him your dislikes, that He may help you to conquer them; talk to Him of your temptations, that He may shield you from them; show Him the wounds of your heart that He may heal them. . . . Tell Him how self-love makes you unjust to others, how vanity tempts you to be insincere, how pride disguises you to yourself and others.

In other words, tell God everything—both good and bad—with an attitude of openness and spontaneity.

Spontaneity in prayer requires a willingness to abandon your own agenda and adopt God's. It means being flexible, looking for good opportunities no matter what comes your way. Some of the best times I've ever experienced in and out of prayer have come when I was willing to do something spontaneous in a situation that might otherwise have been boring or negative. For example, I enjoy watching baseball, and for many years I've been a season ticket holder for San Diego Padres games. A few years ago, I went to a game during a season when the Padres were playing very poorly. And this game was typical of that season. By the fourth inning, the team was behind by about eight or nine runs. Everyone in the stands was getting demoralized. Even when all-star Tony Gwynn came up to bat, people barely paid attention—and he usually gets a strong ovation every time his name is mentioned on the loudspeaker.

As I sat there in a sea of miserable people, I got an idea. The next time the vendor came by, I bought bags of popcorn for everyone in my section. I grabbed a bunch of bags and then we began tossing them out to people. Everyone loved it. Their spirits began to rise, a camaraderie developed in the section, and everyone started warming up. The Padres didn't get much better after that, but we did. Our area became the cheering section of the stadium.

Spontaneity and creativity in prayer go hand in hand. Sometimes creativity helps in planning special prayer times, such as a day alone with God where you travel to a favorite place, like the outdoors or a hotel, to spend the day in prayer and praise. Other times creativity can help you with your day-to-day prayer arrangements. Fred Rowe is a prayer partner and friend with a busy schedule. He is a psychiatrist and has a family with three small boys. He has used his creativity to make sure that he can have a prayer time every morning. He generally gets up at 4:30 in the morning and goes for a drive. His hour in the car is his quiet time. As he drives, he praises and prays, allowing God to dictate the agenda.

I've experienced a lot of blessings from God because of a willingness to be spontaneous. Probably the greatest have been my early morning prayer times. Since 1972, rarely has a week gone by when I haven't awakened at least once between two and three o'clock in the morning. Each time, if I can't fall back to sleep within fifteen minutes, I assume that God wants to speak to me, and I get out of bed and go to my office downstairs. I get out a pen, legal pad, and Bible, and I spend the remaining hours of the night with Him. Sometimes when I sit and pray, I hear very little. Other times He speaks to me so fast through ideas that I can hardly get them written down fast enough.

One night while I was in Atlanta to teach a conference, God woke me up in my hotel room. I couldn't get back to sleep, so I got up, grabbed my legal pad, and started praying. God gave me only two words that whole night: "Lead and intercede." That was all, just those two words. He was reminding me of the two responsibilities that He wanted me to focus on as a pastor.

Being awakened in the wee hours of the morning is not very convenient. And the setting isn't always the greatest. But some of the best things I've experienced in life and the greatest ideas I've ever had have come out of those spontaneous times alone with God in the middle of the night.

2. Be Specific

The second attitude to adopt toward prayer is the desire to be direct and specific with God. Jesus warns us in Matthew 6:7, "And when you pray, do not keep on babbling like pagans, for they think they will be heard because of their many words." It's not the number of words you say or how eloquent you are that counts with God. As we speak, it is the sincerity of our words that matters to God. What is in our hearts gives our voices credibility.

I recently read an article that came from the Colorado Legal Secretaries Association that shows how a simple message can be distorted by unnecessary words. It contained a version of one line of the Lord's Prayer—worded as if it had been written by an attorney:

> We respectfully petition, request, and entreat that due and adequate provision be made, this day and date first above and inscribed, for the satisfying of petitioner's nutritional requirements

and for the organizing of such methods of allocation and distribution as may be deemed necessary and proper to assure the reception by and for said petitioner's of such quantity of cereal products (hereinafter called "bread") as shall in the judgment of the aforesaid petitioners constitute a sufficient amount.

In other words, "Give us this day our daily bread" (At seventy-seven words, this rewritten line is longer than the entire Lord's Prayer, which is only fifty-six words!)

The most effective forms of communication are brief and to the point. For example, just look at some of the great works from our history as a nation. The Gettysburg Address, for example, is only 297 words long, and it's considered one of the greatest speeches ever delivered in the English language. The Declaration of Independence, the document the newly born United States used to sever its ties with powerful Great Britain, is only 300 words. Contrast this with one government order setting the price of cabbage, which reportedly contained 26,911 words!

Besides being direct with God, we should also be as specific as we can. How many times have you prayed something like, "God bless America, bless our church, bless our missionaries . . ." or simply "God be with us"?

Specific prayer has power. Remember, Jesus says that you will be given whatever you ask for in His name (John 16:23-24). So take a look at some examples of how you can pray more effectively:

Instead of praying . . .	Pray this . . .
God, save this country.	Save my neighbor, Bobby, by bringing him to Christ.
God, help me to do well in school.	Help me to study well and make an A on this next test.
God, bless my pastor.	Anoint my pastor to preach salvation this Sunday.

Instead of praying . . .	Pray this . . .
God, teach people to love each other.	Help me to love my wife and make her feel loved.
God, be with us.	Teach me Your will in this area and help me obey You.

Being specific in prayer has another benefit. When God gives us an answer, we know it. We can know it when our neighbor gets saved. We can see people come to Christ during the Sunday sermon. We can ask our spouses if our actions make them feel loved. And not only that—when we ask God to be involved in our lives in specific ways, it gives Him the chance to tell us how we need to change ourselves. The more specific we are in our requests, the more alert we will be to answers when they come—and the more specific we can be with our thanks and praises to God later on.

3. ASK the Right Way

Part of any good relationship is a sensitivity to the other person and their needs. In our relationship with God, it's obvious that He already knows our needs. As Jesus said in Matthew 6:8, "Your Father knows what you need before you ask him." But how well do we know what God wants for us? Ironically, we know ourselves less well than God does. Ford Philpot said, "Too many of us want what we don't need and need what we don't want."

We have to learn to put ourselves at the disposal of God's agenda. Too often we plug away at ours, blind to what God has for us. Many times God mercifully withholds His answers to our prayers until we come to Him with the right request. Ruth Graham, wife of evangelist Billy Graham, once said, "God has not always answered my prayers. If He had, I would have married the wrong man—several times."

God has many incredible, wonderful things for us, if only we ask for them. But if we don't ask for them, how can God give them to us (James 4:2)? Someone once said, "Heaven is filled with a room that will surprise all of us when we see it. It has within it large boxes, neatly packaged with lovely ribbons and our name on top. They are things never delivered to earth because they were never requested."

How do we learn to ask the right questions? Jesus said, "Ask and it will be given to you; seek and you will find; knock and the door will be opened to you. For everyone who asks receives; he who seeks finds; and to him who knocks, the door will be opened" (Matt. 7:7-8).

I've found that the acronym "ASK" (ask, seek, and knock) helps to remind me how to make requests of God in a way that pleases Him. I believe it may help you too:

ASK: When we approach God and ask Him for something, it implies that we have a need that we want met. So if we want to ask Him the right questions, we should first examine our needs. If they are genuine and in accordance with God's will, then we can ask with pure motives, and that's crucial to having our prayers answered (James 4:3).

As you prepare to approach God to ask Him for something, answer the following questions. They will help you examine your needs and better direct your requests:

1. Is my request fair and helpful to everyone concerned?
2. Is my request in harmony with the Word of God?
3. Will it blend with my gifts?
4. Will it draw me closer to God?
5. What is my part in answering this prayer?

If you are able to examine yourself and your requests honestly, this frees God to work in you when your requests aren't pure and to answer them when they are.

SEEK: When people seek, as Jesus directs us to do, they are asking with effort. This implies that He expects us to do our part, even as we ask Him to do His. So when Jesus teaches us to pray, "Give us this day our daily bread," He doesn't mean that we are to sit back and expect God to rain down manna from heaven on us. After all, Scripture says that a person who will not work shall not eat (2 Thess. 3:10). What Jesus means is, "Give us the opportunity to earn our bread." God does not give added resources to those who are lazy.

Prayer without action is presumption. When we pray, we are to invest ourselves, just as Jesus taught us in the parable of the talents. As a result, there is a return on our investment, and God agrees to give us even more. As it says in Matthew 25:29, "Everyone who has will be given more, and he will have an abundance. Whoever does not have, even what he has will be taken from him."

There is a saying that you've probably heard: "He who prays and prays, but acts not on what he knows, is like the man who plans and plans but never sows." I've found that to be true. God will not do what only He can do, until we do all that we can do. So when we pray, we need to be ready to do our part.

KNOCK: When Jesus directs us to knock, He's asking us to be persistent. The Amplified version of the Matthew 7:7-8 passage makes this very clear: "Keep on asking and it will be given you; keep on seeking and you will find; keep on knocking [reverently] and the door will be opened to you. For everyone who keeps on asking receives, and he who keeps on seeking finds, and to him who keeps on knocking, the door will be opened."

I was once visited by a lady in my congregation. She had been asking God to bring her unsaved brother to Christ for a couple of months, and she was getting impatient because he still hadn't made a commitment to follow Jesus.

"Pastor," she asked, "how long must I keep on praying?"

"Until the answer comes," I answered.

That is what God wants from us. Whenever our prayers are unanswered, God wants us to continue praying until the answer comes or He changes our request. And that is what always happens. An answer comes or God changes our heart and prayer. For example, look at the case of Abraham and Sarah in the Old Testament. They prayed for a child, and God answered their prayer—decades later than they expected, but He answered it. And in the case of Paul, do you remember how he prayed over and over for God to remove his "thorn in the flesh"? After Paul prayed the third time, God said, "My grace is sufficient for you, for my power is made perfect in weakness" (2 Cor. 12:9). It was then that Paul realized that the thorn was there for a reason, and he changed his prayer. He aligned his own will with that of God, and he learned to be content.

One of the most frustrating things for many people is having to wait for an answer from God. I know that because I have a choleric temperament. I evaluate situations very quickly and make decisions even faster, so I especially dislike waiting. But God doesn't ask us to be persistent to tease us or to withhold things from us. He does it because He wants us to grow in our relationship with Him. He wants us to be completely yielded to Him.

In the first few years that I was the senior pastor at Skyline Wesleyan Church in San Diego, California, the church began to grow substantially. It quickly became obvious to me that it wouldn't be long before we would need a larger facility. And since enlarging on the current property wasn't an option, that meant we would need to relocate.

When I was a pastor in Indiana and we had a similar problem, I got together with my board, developed a strategy, and we were off. Within a couple of days we got someone to donate the land, another person to contribute materials, and we were ready to build. But it's a whole different ball game in southern California. Land is very expensive, and it isn't easy to find. So I got together with my board, we formed a relocation committee, and they began searching for some land.

After many months of searching, they found a parcel of land that looked perfect for us: thirty acres for $2 million—a pretty good price for San Diego (we could have bought half the county back in Indiana for that price). And we were happy with the location, too. But before we were to make a decision about it, I took my prayer partners there on a Saturday to walk and pray over the land. It didn't take long in prayer before we had a unanimous sense that this was not the land God wanted for our church. So we let the opportunity to purchase it go by, and we continued to pray, knowing that there must be some reason why God said no.

A few months later, God opened the doors for another plot of land. It was eighty acres right on the freeway near a new subdivision with hundreds of young, unchurched families. We ended up purchasing that land for $1.8 million—less than we would have paid for the thirty-acre parcel. And on top of that, through a series of miracles, Skyline ended up with 120 acres of land instead of eighty for that price.

God honored our persistence and greatly blessed our obedience. And He will do the same for you. When you pray, don't give up. Maintain a positive attitude and continue to ask, seek, and knock.

4. Pray with All Your Heart

Have you ever tried to maintain a conversation with a toddler? While you're in the middle of a sentence, they figure it's a good time to play with one of their toys, chase after the dog, or look for that piece of cheese they stuck between the cushions of the sofa the night before. It's really hard to keep their attention for more than a couple of minutes.

That's probably how God feels when He is trying to communicate with us. Many people pray for a minute here or there during their busy days, giving God their attention for only a moment. Praying throughout the day is good, but we also need to set aside some time every day where we can focus on God and give Him our full attention. The problem is that even then we have a hard time focusing. It's the war of the wandering thoughts. As we pray, we think about the grocery list; the dog or the kids distract us; or we realize the bedroom needs cleaning. It turns out we're as bad as toddlers when it comes to paying attention to God.

In all honesty, most people battle with this problem. Ours is a world of distractions, many of which try to divide our attention. But it's a battle we need to continue fighting. When we approach God, we must strive to give Him all of our heart, not just a part of it. God doesn't answer the prayer of the double-minded person (James 1:8).

Part of the solution is to come to prayer with the right attitude with the desire to give Him all of our attention, just as Jesus suggests in Matthew 6:6. But there are also tools and techniques that can help us to keep focused:

PRAY ALOUD: Probably the simplest way to help you focus is to pray aloud. It actually makes it difficult for your mind to wander. Try it. You may at first feel a little self-conscious, but you'll soon get used to it.

WRITE DOWN THE DISTRACTIONS: For some people, the biggest distraction to prayer comes as they think about all the things they need to do that day. To solve that problem, as you pray, keep paper and a pen close by and write down each task as it comes to you and then forget about it until later. And if you still can't help thinking about it, then take it to God in prayer. Distractions are things you need either to take out of God's way or need to take directly to God.

KEEP A PRAYER JOURNAL: Journaling is also a good

tool because it keeps the mind focused on the task at hand. There are dozens of ways to use one to help you: You can write out prayers, outline them, or jot down key thoughts or Scripture verses. Use whatever works best for you.

The additional value of journaling is that it provides a record of your growing relationship with God, gives insight into your growth, clarifies your thoughts and requests, provides a record of answered prayers, and indicates recurring issues in your life. As Douglas J. Rumford said in "The Value of a Personal Journal," "As we learn to trust our insights, a creative power builds momentum: ideas begin to propel themselves into our consciousness. Frequently, the seeds of sermons or particular actions are planted when we break ground with a journal."

I once read a quote that describes well the condition of many Christians' prayer lives. Francois Fenelon said in his book, *Christian Perfection*, "Too many people pray like little boys who knock at doors, then run away." Being unable to give your whole heart to God is a serious obstacle to building a strong relationship with Him. Just as the moon cannot be reflected by a restless sea, God cannot be experienced by an unquiet mind. But having a regular time where you give God your full attention in prayer grows your relationship with Him in a powerful way. It's the difference between running after knocking at the door, and going in and getting to know God. The latter changes your life.

5. Pray Continually

When you've begun learning to pray with all your heart, prayer begins to overflow into more of your life. In 1 Thessalonians 5:17, Paul tells believers to "pray continually." And by that he means that we should maintain an almost continuous conversation with God throughout the day—like breathing, constant and life giving. Once your relationship with God begins to deepen, that becomes easier to do.

Growing up, I learned about praying continually (or as we called it, praying without ceasing) from my father, who has always been a great role model for me. For him, praying was as natural as breathing or talking to my mom. He always seemed to be talking as he walked through the house—but he wasn't talking to himself. He was talking to God. Sometimes when we were riding in the car, he'd just start a conversation with God. Dad taught me to praise Him when something good happened; ask Him questions when I was confused; cry to Him when I was hurt; and thank Him when I was blessed. And any time we had to make a decision, Dad's first words were always, "Let's just stop right now and pray about it." Dad and Mom taught me that the most effective and contented Christians made prayer a part of their lifestyles.

Developing a strong relationship with God through prayer is not something that happens overnight. But it can happen if a person approaches it with the right attitude and is willing to give it the time and energy it requires. Aristotle said, "Wishing to be friends is quick work, but friendship is a slow-ripening fruit."

But what in this life—and for eternity—could be better than developing a relationship with a Father who loves us perfectly and who wants to know us and grow us into the people He created us to be? I can't think of anything that compares with that. And the way to make it happen is through prayer.

DISCUSSION QUESTIONS

1. Growing up, with which of your relatives did you have the best relationship? What made that relationship so special?

2. What do you consider to be the most important qualities in a positive, growing relationship?

3. Discuss ideas for things to do to improve a close relationship and help it grow. Include some of the things you are currently doing to build your relationship with your spouse, child, or close friend. Can any of those same things be used to improve your relationship with God?

4. When you pray, which of the following is most difficult?
   a. being spontaneous
   b. being specific
   c. asking the right way (ask, seek, knock)
   d. praying with all your heart
   e. praying continually

5. Identify one thing you can begin doing immediately to help you with your most difficult prayer area. Break into groups of two or three and pray for one another in these areas.

3

DEVELOPING PRACTICAL PRAYER SKILLS

Yet those who wait for the LORD
Will gain new strength;
They will mount up with wings like eagles,
They will run and not get tired,
They will walk and not become weary.
Isaiah 40:31 (NASB)

L ess than a year after I accepted the call to preach at age seventeen, I enrolled in Circleville Bible College to prepare for the ministry. My experience there was very positive. I learned a lot, made new friends, began preaching for the first time, and participated in many other activities. But one of the most important things I learned there was how to have a deep devotional time with God. It was something that I didn't learn in school; I learned it by spending an hour with God every day. And my life has never been the same since.

I used to finish my classes by noon, and then I'd spend lunchtime in the cafeteria with my friends. But every day at one o'clock in the afternoon, I'd leave them, grab my Bible and a legal pad, and head across campus. My destination was an old block building that sat in a field out back of the college campus. I think it had once been a utility shed, but it looked like it hadn't been used in over a dozen years.

The trip from the cafeteria to that old shed was only about a quarter of a mile, but some days it seemed longer, because I just couldn't get there fast enough. My spirit used to soar as I anticipated the time I was going to spend with God, getting to know Him and being close to Him in prayer. Every day for four years I met with God in that field.

Two weeks after I graduated from college, Margaret and I got married. And two weeks after that, I was in my first pastorate at a small church in Hillham, Indiana. We moved into a tiny house there on a small forty-acre farm. The first thing I did after we moved in was search for a place where I could go to pray. And I immediately found one—a huge rock just inside of the woods behind our house. I used to scramble up to the top of that rock and spend some incredible times with God there.

Now I look back at the time when I was learning to spend an hour with God, and I can say with all honesty that is when I grew the most spiritually. I certainly continue to grow now, and the time I currently spend with God is deep and rewarding. But in those early days I sensed that God was rapidly changing me, helping me develop into the person He wanted me to be. And it was then that He really began using me in work for His kingdom.

God can do the same thing with you. Don't think that you have to start by spending a whole hour with Him daily, although that is a worthy goal. The main thing is that you are consistent, spending a good amount of time with Him every day. When you do, instead of looking at Sunday as the day you catch up with God and get reacquainted with Him, the times of worship at church will be icing on the cake—because you will have been with Him all week long, talking with Him and getting to know Him, growing and developing.

BAG LUNCH OR BANQUET

The difference between quickly throwing up a few prayers when you have a moment, and spending a quality devotion time with God is like the difference between buying fast food and dining in a fine restaurant. With fast food, you drive up, yell into a microphone, and drive around to a window where they throw you a sack of food. But in a fine restaurant, you sit down. You spend time in pleasant conversation with your table companion, and you become nourished and refreshed. It's a rewarding experience for mind, body, and soul.

Many Christians have only had spiritual fast food in their lives; they've never experienced the banquet God has for them. I've found that there are two main reasons people miss out on great prayer times with God:

1. LACK OF DESIRE: To develop a regular devotion time, you have to really want to do it. Many people complain that they lack time. But if they were really honest with themselves, they'd realize that you make time for what you truly care about. If you really want to spend time praying, you give up something else, and just do it.

If lack of desire is keeping you from developing a deep daily time with God, stop what you're doing and pray for it *right now*. If you ask God for the desire, He will give it to you.

2. NO PRACTICAL STRATEGY FOR DAILY PRAYER: The idea of spending an extended daily time with God is very intimidating to a lot of people. When you talk about watching television for an hour, that doesn't sound like very much time. But if you ask someone unused to praying to spend an hour with God, sixty minutes sounds like a lifetime. However, if you approach your daily time with a good strategy, you can develop a quality devotion time that's not only rewarding, but life-changing.

GAME PLAN FOR A DAILY DEVOTION

There's not a single right way to have a devotion time with God. Everybody's different, and what works for one person doesn't work for another. But you have to start somewhere. The following ten steps are ones I've developed over the years in my own devotions. They are without a doubt the best approach to prayer for me. My hope is that they will also work for you. Try them out and change them to suit your own needs.

No matter how you plan to structure your devotion time, let me give you one piece of advice. I've observed that there are three ways people enter the presence of God: through prayer, Bible reading, and worship. But everyone's different about which is the best for them. Find out which one of the three draws you to God the most quickly and easily, and always start your devotion time with it.

1. Preparation Time

In order to have a good devotion time, you need to prepare yourself at the beginning—physically, mentally, emotionally, and spiritually. The physical preparation is the easiest. Find yourself a comfortable location where you won't be distracted. Bring with you any resources you might need. I always have on hand my Bible, a legal pad and pen, a hymnal, and (when possible) pictures of the people I'm going to pray for. I know others who take a cassette player to play worship music. Others write using their computer. Do whatever's best for you. The idea is to have at hand anything that will help you. At the very least, you will want to have a Bible with you and something to write on.

Once you've found the right place and gotten your material together, get comfortable. Do whatever feels natural to you. If you like to sit, then sit. If you feel more comfortable walking, then do that. If you'd prefer to kneel, that's great. Or you can change around according to your mood or to how God is speaking to you. Most of the time I sit, but when I get really excited, I walk. The main idea is for you to be ready to meet with God.

Once you've settled in, prepare yourself mentally, emotionally, and spiritually by focusing on God. Some people go into prayer time as if they were stepping up to a negotiation table, but that's not how we should approach God. Begin by declaring your intention to obey whatever He asks you to do. Getting your heart right first prepares you for everything that follows. Start by asking God to help you spend the time with Him profitably, and then allow Him to speak to you.

It's at this time that you will begin your devotion time with prayer, worship, or Scripture reading, depending on which one is best for you. No matter which you do first, be sure not to do all the talking. Leave plenty of quiet times where God can talk to you. Remember, your agenda is to get where God is and hear what He has to say to you.

2. Waiting Time

Isaiah 40:31 has a wonderful promise for those who wait upon God. It says, "Yet those who wait for the LORD / Will gain new strength; / They will mount up with wings like eagles, / They will run and not get tired, / They will walk and not become weary" (NASB). God honors those who wait on Him. Most people spend way too much time in prayer talking and not enough listening. They talk so much that they miss out on the best part of a personal prayer time.

Overall, I try to spend about 20 percent of my time talking and 80 percent of my time listening. That waiting time is not a period where I'm just zoning out. I wait actively. The word *wait* in the

Isaiah passage means waiting with expectation; it's active, not passive. When we wait on God, we are to listen with the expectation that He will speak to us in a meaningful way.

As you wait for God, allow Him to do three things with you:

- **LET GOD LOVE YOU:** God is always waiting to tell you He loves you, every minute of every day. That's true because you have value, thanks to Jesus Christ. By letting God express His love, you are allowing Him to build your self-esteem spiritually. Allow yourself mentally to sit on Jesus' lap or cry on His shoulder, and let His unconditional love touch your heart.
- **LET GOD SEARCH YOU:** Once you know that God loves you, and that He will continue to love you no matter what you've done, it becomes possible for you to let Him search you. Allowing Him to do that can be difficult at first, but it's crucial to the development of your relationship.
- **LET GOD SHOW YOU:** God will prepare you for the day ahead if you allow Him to. The best way to do that is to give the day to Him during your waiting time. He can then show you His heart—how He cares for people and wants to minister to them. And when you know God's heart, you can show it to others.

Waiting and listening can be difficult. They are not things most people do well today, because we live in an instant society. But you can learn to do them if you persevere. And the reward is incredible; when you listen for God's voice, you will eventually hear it.

3. Confession Time

Unconfessed sin is a roadblock to answered prayer. But a good, honest waiting time naturally leads into a time of confession before

God. If you let Him search you, He will point out what you need to confess. And in confessing, you will once again restore your relationship with Him (I discuss this issue more in the next chapter).

Here are five things to keep in mind about confession:

- **CONFESS SIN IMMEDIATELY:** Unconfessed sin drives a wedge between God and us, so the sooner we confess it, the better off we are. Whenever you sin, confess as soon as possible—don't wait for Sunday or even your daily prayer time. Do it right then and there.

  I learned this lesson at age seventeen. Just three days after rededicating my life to Christ, I was at basketball practice when I went up for a rebound and came down on another player's foot. I felt my ankle roll over and pop. As I fell to the ground, I cussed using the Lord's name.

  I had told everyone on the team about my commitment, and I had already started witnessing to them. When Chet Irey, a fellow player, heard what I said, he turned to me and said, "John, I thought you were a Christian. What are you doing talking like that?"

  I felt terrible, and I realized that I had made an awful mistake. As they put me on the training table and iced my ankle, right then and there I prayed to God for forgiveness.

- **NEVER ALLOW YOUR POSITION TO KEEP YOU FROM CONFESSING SIN:** No matter who you are, what you do, or what your position is in the church, you are never above the need to confess sin and pray for forgiveness. If you ever think you are, you're in really big trouble.

- **GOD IS NEVER SURPRISED BY WHAT WE DO, SO BE HONEST:** You can't keep anything from God, and you certainly can't hurt His feelings by telling Him your mistakes, so you'd better be honest with Him.

When you aren't, you're fooling only yourself and hindering the relationship.

- **GOD WILL ALWAYS TELL US WHEN WE'VE DONE SOMETHING WRONG:** If we have a genuine desire to confess our sins and ask forgiveness, God will tell us when we've done something wrong. No honest Christian ever has to worry about unknown sin in his or her life.

- **WHEN SIN IS TOLERATED, IT INCREASES:** Any time we don't seek forgiveness, and we allow sin to remain in our lives, it increases and continues to do further damage. Sin left unchecked for a long time can eventually consume us.

Confession has wonderful benefits. It clears the air with God and allows you to communicate with Him without encumbrances.

4. Bible Time

I once read a story in *The Employment Counselor* where a young Christian was preparing for a trip when his traveling companion came into the room to see how he was doing.

"Are you done packing?" his friend asked.

"Almost," said the young man. "The only things I have left to pack are a guidebook, a lamp, a mirror, a microscope, a volume of fine poetry, a couple of biographies, a package of old letters, a book of songs, a sword, a hammer, and a set of books I've been reading."

"Where are you going to fit all that stuff?" the friend asked.

"Right here," the young man replied. He reached for his Bible and put it in the corner of his suitcase.

Reading the Bible daily will do awesome things to your walk with God. Second Timothy 3:16-17 says, "All Scripture is God-breathed and is useful for teaching, rebuking, correcting and training in righteousness, so that the man of God may be thoroughly equipped for every good work." When I became serious about learning the Word of God and obeying what it taught, it made an impact on me. But when I learned to *pray* Scripture, that's when the Word really came alive to me. And my prayers gained new power, because I was praying using God's Word, which is eternal (Ps. 119:89).

For a long time I took for granted that most Christians knew how to pray Scripture. I discovered my error at a prayer partners' retreat several years ago. That year, when I prayed for my prayer partners, which I always do, I prayed a passage of Scripture. They were incredibly touched by the Holy Spirit and said it was one of the most powerful prayer times they'd ever experienced. Most had never done anything like it before. And that's when I decided that I needed to teach it to my board and everyone in my congregation.

Let me also teach you how to pray Scripture. Begin by selecting a passage from the Bible that speaks to your heart on the subject you want to pray about. To pray the passage, just personalize it as you read it, applying what it says to yourself or to the person you're praying for. Respond to the passage mentally, emotionally, and spiritually, and feel free to stop reading and continue praying as God's Spirit prompts you. You will find that it changes your life. Any time you pray God's will and His promises back to Him, you'll receive special blessings from Him.

Let me show you an example of how to pray Scripture. Here's a passage straight out of Philippians:

> **Rejoice in the Lord always. I will say it again: Rejoice! Let your gentleness be evident to all. The Lord is near. Do not be anxious about anything, but in everything, by prayer and petition, with thanksgiving, present your requests to God. And the peace of God, which transcends all under-**

standing, will guard your hearts and your minds in Christ Jesus. (4:4–7)

And here is the Scripture in the form of a prayer:

> Heavenly Father, *I rejoice in You always. I will say it again: I rejoice!* You are an awesome, incredible God. *I pray that my* gentleness, *which comes from the power of Your Holy Spirit, would be evident to all.* Lord, *I know You are near.* You have promised never to forsake or abandon me. *And for that reason, I will not be anxious about anything.* You are on the throne, and I will trust in You. *In everything, Lord, by prayer and petition, with thanksgiving and praise, I will present my requests to You.* And Lord, I ask that Your peace, *which transcends all understanding, will guard my heart and mind in Christ Jesus* from the cares and anxieties of this day. *It is in the strong name of Your Son, Jesus Christ, that I pray. Amen.*

Once you've learned to pray Scripture and have made it a regular part of your devotion time, it will become difficult for you *not* to pray Scripture any time you read the Bible. You'll find that as a verse makes a strong impression on you, you'll stop reading and begin praying the passage and applying it to yourself or others. It's truly transforming.

I taught my congregation how to do this by praying Scripture over them in a Sunday service. It was one of the most moving services I've ever led. They went away from that time as new people. You can too. If you've never prayed Scripture before, try it. You'll be amazed by how it changes and empowers your prayer life.

5. Meditation Time

James advises believers not to just listen to God's Word but to do what it says (James 1:22). The step that helps bridge the gap between reading and acting is meditation, because it helps us understand Scripture and apply it to our lives. Psalm 1:1-2 says:

> **Blessed is the man**
> **who does not walk in the counsel of the wicked**
> **or stand in the way of sinners**
> **or sit in the seat of mockers.**
> **But his delight is in the law of the LORD,**
> **and on his law he meditates day and night.**
> **He is like a tree planted by streams of water,**
> **which yields its fruit in season**
> **and whose leaf does not wither.**
> **Whatever he does prospers.**

Meditating on God's Word is simply thinking about it with the desire to discover its truth and apply it to your life. For example, let's say you are reading Ephesians 4:1, which says,

"As a prisoner for the Lord, then, I urge you to live a life worthy of the calling you have received." As you begin to meditate on the verse, you might begin thinking about your calling and the purpose God has planned for you. Maybe you aren't sure about your purpose, which causes you to ask God what it is. Or if you know what God has called you to do, you might start examining your life to see if you're living in a way that God would consider worthy. Just thinking about it may prompt you to renew your obedience to God's vision. There's no telling where God will lead you once you begin to think about His Word and apply it to your life.

Meditation has many benefits: It helps you examine your relationship with God, see yourself in a right way, and discover where you are in your spiritual journey. And, of course, it helps you better understand how to obey. The process can be painful or exciting, but it always brings you closer to God.

6. Intercession Time

Intercession is praying for others, and it's an important part of a good daily devotion time. In Paul's first letter to Timothy, he gives clear instructions on how we should pray for others. He says:

> **I urge, then, first of all, that requests, prayers, intercession and thanksgiving be made for everyone—for kings and all those in authority, that we may live peaceful and quiet lives in all godliness and holiness. This is good, and pleases God our Savior, who wants all men to be saved and to come to a knowledge of the truth. (2:1-4)**

Intercessory prayer clearly pleases God and is expected to be a part of our daily lives. Plus it helps us to know God's heart.

For me, intercession has usually been the longest part of my devotion time with God. As a pastor, my two primary jobs were to equip the saints and intercede for the people. That was a big job with a congregation of over three thousand. But to facilitate this process, I used to pray visually for the people. I always had the church directory close by during my devotions and looked at the pictures of the families I was praying for. And I also had a system for the newer people in church. Periodically I'd ask people to allow the ushers and greeters to take Polaroid photos of them. Then I'd have them put the people's names on the pictures, hole-punch them, and put them on huge key rings. Then I'd pray through those pictures too.

Intercession is an important part of our devotion time. It not only benefits others and connects us to God, but it also helps us. As the Jewish proverb says, "He who prays for his neighbor will be heard for himself." More than that, intercession is at the heart of partnering with your pastor in prayer. And for that reason, I will talk about it in greater detail in chapter 5.

7. Petition Time

Once you've spent time listening to God, confessing your sins, reading and meditating on His Word, and asking Him to bless others, then you are ready to ask God to see to your personal needs. He wants you to bring everything to Him—all of your physical, emotional, and spiritual needs. And He wants you to do it with the right heart.

As you bring your list of needs and desires to God, keep these things in mind:

- **PRAY WITH THE ATTITUDE OF "THY WILL BE DONE":** When we pray for others, our motives are usually good. But when we pray for ourselves, our emotions and thoughts get caught up with the issues, and our motives are not always pure. Praying "Thy will be done" purifies our motives and aligns our will with God's.

  Praying for God's will is not a show of weakness or lack of faith. When Jesus prayed, "Not my will, but yours be done" (Luke 22:42), He was submitting His will to God's. Any time we *demand* things from God, we only show immaturity. Ironically, those who are spiritually mature come to God with childlike faith.

  Our prayers should ask God to help us do what He is blessing, not bless what we are doing. God is not as interested in our circumstances as He is in our attitude. When our attitude is right, our prayers become consistent with His will and ultimately benefit us—often in ways far greater than we could have planned or imagined.

  This prayer, attributed to a civil war soldier, says it well:

I asked God for strength, that I might achieve.
I was made weak, that I might learn humbly to obey. . .

I asked for health, that I might do great things.
I was given infirmity, that I might do better things. . .
I asked for riches, that I might be happy.
I was given poverty, that I might be wise. . .
I asked for power, that I might have the praise of men.
I was given weakness, that I might feel the need of God. . .
I asked for all things, that I might enjoy life.
I was given life, that I might enjoy all things. . .
I got nothing that I asked for—
but everything I had hoped for.
Almost despite myself, my unspoken prayers were answered.
I am, among all men, most richly blessed!

- **BE HONEST WITH YOUR FEELINGS, PROBLEMS, AND NEEDS:** Even though God already knows everything you need and everything you feel, He still wants you to come to Him, and He wants you to do it openly and honestly. There is nothing wrong with expressing your true emotions in prayer. In fact it's appropriate because it deepens our relationship with God. He always meets us right where we are.

- **TALK TO GOD ABOUT THE LITTLE THINGS THAT CONCERN YOU:** I've often heard people say, "I only talk to God about the important stuff. I don't want to bother Him with the little things." I'm amused by that. Can you think of anything in your life that isn't little compared to God? Yet He says that He knows when the sparrow falls and even the number of hairs on our heads (Matt. 10:29-30). I wonder how often we miss the best God has for us because we try to work out all the little things for ourselves. Don't miss out on what God has for you by not sharing everything with Him.

8. Application Time

Application time is where listening and obedience come together as action. There is no better way to demonstrate love for God than by following through with an obedient response to what He asks of us. As Jesus said, "If anyone loves me, he will obey my teaching. My Father will love him, and we will come to him and make our home with him. He who does not love me will not obey my teaching. These words you hear are not my own; they belong to the Father who sent me" (John 14:23-24).

God sometimes asks things of His people that are unusual and defy our understanding. For example, the prophet Jeremiah had God make a strange request of him. He was in prison in Jerusalem right when the city was about to be overrun by the Babylonians. At that time, God told him to buy some land there. It wasn't exactly a great time to buy real estate since the enemy was about to take everybody and everything away from the city.

Despite the peculiarity of God's instructions to him, Jeremiah obeyed immediately and completely (Jer. 32). He bought the field, and God used his actions as a symbol of hope to the people—that they would some day be restored to Jerusalem. That's the kind of response God wants to see in us. Partial obedience is really disobedience. If we are going to obey, we need to do it all the way.

Every single time I've met with God in prayer, He has never failed to ask something of me—that's why I always have a legal pad with me when I pray. But God never overwhelms me with His instructions. He usually gives me only one thing to do at a time. (Occasionally He'll give me two; very rarely does He give me three.) He may ask me to intercede for someone. He may tell me to spend more time with one of the children. Or He may give me a message to preach. But no matter wnat He tells me to do, He does it clearly and simply so that it's not difficult for me to understand or obey.

And once I've followed through on that one thing, He gives me the next thing.

Obedience is key in the development of your relationship with God. If your spiritual growth has come to a standstill and you're not sure why, check yourself. You may be bogged down in disobedience. Only when you follow through on what God has asked of you can you move forward in your spiritual journey.

9. Faith Time

Praying in faith is my favorite part of any devotion time. Hebrews 11:1 says, "Now faith is being sure of what we hope for and certain of what we do not see." Faith prayer is a verbal expression of faith, confirming the expectation that God can and will bring about desired results to accomplish His purposes. It's like thanking God in advance for what He intends to do.

I learned about praying in faith from my father, who did it all the time when I was growing up. I especially remember one trip with him when I was in the school quartet at Circleville Bible College. Dad was the college president at the time, and when we performed at churches, he sometimes traveled with us and preached the sermon.

On this occasion we went to a small rural church that hadn't experienced growth in years. As we set up for the performance, we met with the church's pastor, a downtrodden man who seemed to be devoid of hope. "I don't know why you're going to all this trouble," he said. "Nobody's been saved in this church for five years."

After we finished setting up, we got together for our usual prayer time. My dad closed our time of prayer by saying this:

> Lord, I know You will do great things in this church tonight. You say in Isaiah 55:11 that Your word that goes forth out of Your mouth shall not return unto You void, but shall accomplish that which

pleases You, and shall prosper in the thing whereto You sent it. And Lord, we thank You that tonight Your word will accomplish Your purpose. People will be saved and come into Your kingdom this very night. Thank You, Lord, for Your promise and the power of Your Holy Spirit working in and through us. In the name of Jesus we pray, amen.

Dad's faith and the power of the Holy Spirit did a wonderful work that night. Many people were saved in that little church.

Praying in faith is exciting. As long as we pray with right motives, according to God's will and agenda, and not for our own selfish reasons, God will answer those prayers, and great things will happen.

10. Praise and Thanksgiving Time

Many Christians lump praise and thanksgiving together, not realizing that there's a difference between them. Praise recognizes God for who He is. Thanksgiving recognizes Him for what He has done.

Both praise and thanksgiving are necessary ingredients in our relationship with God. It's usually better to start with praise first, because even during tough times when we don't really feel like thanking God, we can always praise Him for who He is. He's the same every day: loving, patient, kind, giving—He's perfect. So we are never without reasons to praise Him. Once we begin, it doesn't take long for our praise to turn into thanksgiving for what He has done.

Worship in the form of praise and thanksgiving gives God a lot of joy. After all, we were all created to worship God. But it also benefits us greatly. When we praise God, He inhabits us. When we thank God, He blesses us. And our worship gives us a better perspective. Paul Billheimer said, "Here is one of the greatest values of praise: It decentralizes self. The worship and praise of God demands a shift of center from self to God. One cannot praise God without relinquishing occupation with self. Praise produces forgetfulness of self and forgetfulness of self is health." When we worship God, it sets the order of things right. After all, we worship God, not because He's blessed us, but because He is God and is worthy of all praise.

Prayer has become an inseparable part of my life and the reason for any success I've achieved. Every major milestone of growth I've experienced has come as the result of God touching me during times of prayer. I believe those milestones never would have happened had I not been spending regular times alone with God.

As you know, finding a good place to be alone with God was an important step for me in developing a strong devotional life, and I had great success in finding good spots, until I moved on to my second pastorate in Lancaster, Ohio. I couldn't find anyplace like the Hillham rock near my home. The best I could find was a place in Rising Park, which was a fifteen-minute drive from where we lived. Because of the distance, I couldn't go there every day. But whenever I could, I'd drive across to the park and spend the whole afternoon sitting on a rocky ledge with a view of the entire city of Lancaster. I had some wonderful times with God in that park

During those years, I often prayed for my brother, Larry. He lived nearby right in Lancaster, and I talked to God about him constantly. He wasn't walking with the Lord back in those days, and I was worried about him.

Early one morning before I left to go to work, I heard a truck rumble up the street and stop in front of our house, and then there was a knock at the door. When I opened it, I was surprised to see Larry standing there grinning.

"I want you to see something, John," he said. "Come on."

He turned around and I followed him out into the front yard.

There on the street was parked a huge flatbed truck—as big as I'd ever seen. And on that flatbed was a massive rock.

He said, "I know how you like to pray on a rock—so I brought you one."

Larry had some men put that rock in the woods southwest of our house, and once again I had a wonderful place to meet with God close to home. I had some wonderful prayer times there, and whenever I met with God, I never failed to thank Him for Larry, and to intercede for him. And in time, Larry came back to God. Now he's a wonderfully strong Christian businessman who dedicates his time and talents to building God's kingdom.

DISCUSSION QUESTIONS

1. Which brings you most quickly into God's presence: worship, prayer, or Scripture reading? Why does that one speak to you most strongly?

2. What recent event or circumstance would you like to thank God for? What does it tell you about God's character?

3. King David of Israel was said to be a man after God's own heart. His relationship with God remained strong largely because of his prayer life. Read 2 Samuel 12. Based on that passage, what would you say is David's attitude regarding each aspect of prayer mentioned in the chapter?
    a. preparation
    b. waiting
    c. confession
    d. God's Word
    e. meditation
    f. intercession
    g. petition
    h. application (obedience)
    i. faith
    j. praise and thanksgiving

4. Listening is one of the hardest things for many American Christians to do. How effective are you at listening to God? What makes it difficult? What helps make it easier? What can you do to improve?

5. God says that those who love Him will obey Him (John 14:23). Think about the one area where God is currently calling you to obedience. Break into groups of two or three and pray for one another in these areas.

4

AVOIDING PERSONAL PRAYER KILLERS

The prayer of a righteous man is powerful and effective.
James 5:16

When my wife, Margaret, and I were first married, we owned an old Volkswagen Beetle. One cold morning not too long after we bought it, I went outside and got in the car to go to work and it wouldn't start. I turned the key and nothing happened. All I could hear was a faint clicking sound.

Now, I didn't have a clue about cars back then—and I still don't. But fortunately we had a friend who did. He turned the key one time, heard the clicking, and immediately started climbing into the backseat of the car.

"What are you doing?" I asked. "The engine's back here. Even I know that."

"I want to take a look at your battery," he said as he began yanking out the backseat. "In a Bug it's here, under the seat."

He pulled the seat out. And sure enough, there was the battery.

"Here's your problem," he said. "You see these cables? They connect the battery to the engine and its starter. But where the cables connect to the battery it's all corroded." I could see heavy white junk covering the places where he was pointing. "That corrosion is blocking the electricity. Your engine's not going to start as long as that stuff's blocking the power."

"Can you fix it?" I asked.

"Sure," he said. "We can get rid of this stuff—no problem."

I watched in amazement as he took a bottle of Coke and poured a little on the battery terminals. The corrosion bubbled away. Then he fooled around with the cables a little bit and said, "Try it now." The car started perfectly, as though nothing had been wrong with it.

Our relationship with God and our prayer life function in a way very similar to how my car did back then. As long as there isn't anything in the way blocking our "connection" to God, we have unlimited power. But when we allow junk to come between us and God, we're dead in the water. And no matter how hard or how often we "turn the key" in prayer, we have no power.

10 COMMON PRAYER KILLERS

The best way to keep from having spiritual junk hinder your prayer life is to avoid it. But when you haven't, the best thing to do is clean it up as soon as possible. I've found that there are ten very common blocks to effective prayer. I call them prayer killers because they take away all power from our prayers and hinder our relationship with God. If you find that one or more of these blocks apply to you, confess them to God and ask for His forgiveness to reestablish your connection with Him.

Prayer Killer #1: Unconfessed Sin

Unconfessed sin is probably the most common prayer killer. Psalm 66:18 says, "If I regard wickedness in my heart, the Lord will not hear" (NASB). When the Scripture talks about regarding wickedness, it's referring to unconfessed sin. God is perfect and can't abide sin in us. If we knowingly tolerate sin in our lives, it pushes God away from us. As a result, it makes our prayers powerless.

The good news is that when we confess sin, God forgives it, and it's gone. The slate is clean and we are no longer held accountable.

Jeremiah 31:34 says, "For I will forgive their wickedness and will remember their sins no more." Not only are we forgiven, but God chooses to truly forget our sins of the past. At that point our relationship is restored, and our prayers regain their power. Our past actions may still have consequences, but the sin itself is forgiven.

If you have confessed and surrendered a sin to God and continue to sense accusation toward yourself for that sin, it is not God's voice you are hearing. It is Satan, the accuser, attacking you. Always remember, God's forgiveness is complete. First John 1:9 says, "If we confess our sins, he is faithful and just and will forgive us our sins." Don't let Satan accuse you when Christ has set you free.

Unforgiven sin also has other consequences. We could turn around the Scripture from Psalms to say, "If I regard wickedness in my heart, I will not hear God," and it would also be true. Sin dulls our senses and isolates us from God. Look at the case of Adam and Eve: When they sinned, they didn't want to walk with God; they hid from Him.

Besides making us want to run from God, sin also makes us want to isolate ourselves from other believers. In *Life Together,* Dietrich Bonhoeffer wrote:

> Sin demands to have a man by himself. It withdraws him from the community. The more isolated a person is, the more destructive will be the power of sin over him, and the more disastrous is this isolation. Sin wants to remain unknown. It shuns the light. In the darkness of the unexpressed it poisons the whole being of a person.

Sin pushes the person out of the community of believers, and being away from other Christians prevents us from receiving the benefit of accountability. It's a vicious cycle. As the saying goes, prayer prevents us from sin, and sin prevents us from prayer. If you're harboring sin in your life, confess it now and receive God's forgiveness. Clear away what's preventing you from connecting with God.

Prayer Killer #2: Lack of Faith

Lack of faith has an incredibly negative impact on a Christian's life. Without faith, prayer has no power. Even Jesus was powerless to perform any miracles in Nazareth because of the people's lack of faith (Mark 6:1-6).

Jesus' brother James gives some insight into the effect that faithlessness has on prayer. James 1:5-8 says:

> **If any of you lacks wisdom, he should ask God, who gives generously to all without finding fault, and it will be given to him. But when he asks, he must believe and not doubt, because he who doubts is like a wave of the sea, blown and tossed by the wind. That man should not think he will receive anything from the Lord; he is a double-minded man, unstable in all he does.**

What incredible insight this is into the mind of the unfaithful person. The word *double-minded* speaks of a condition where a person is emotionally divided, almost as if he had two souls. That condition makes a person unstable and incapable of hearing from God or receiving His gifts.

Faith is really an issue of trust. Jesus said, "If you believe, you will receive whatever you ask for in prayer" (Matt. 21:22). People are often reluctant to put their full trust in God. Yet every day they trust people without question, displaying a faith that God would love to receive from them. Think about it. People go to doctors whose names they cannot pronounce, receive a prescription they cannot read, take it to a pharmacist they've never even seen, get a medicine they don't understand, and then take it!

Why is it so much easier to trust these unknowns than to trust a God who is faithful and loving in every way? The answer lies in where we place our trust. Many people place their trust in their friends, spouse, money, or themselves. Anything other than God is sure to disappoint, but even the smallest amount of faith can move mountains.

Prayer Killer #3: Disobedience

I remember one afternoon when I was seventeen lying on my bed at home studying my Bible. About a month before, I had rededicated my life to Christ and accepted the call to preach. This day I was working on memorizing 1 John and came across this verse: "Dear friends, if our hearts do not condemn us, we have confidence before God and receive from him anything we ask, because we obey his commands and do what pleases him" (1 John 3:21-23).

All of a sudden it seemed as if God unlocked a door in my mind and something clicked. I was flooded with understanding. I still remember it vividly, because it was one of those special moments of truth that a person experiences at turning points in his life. As I reread the verse, I circled the word *because* in my Bible. I realized that we receive from God *because* we obey Him. That's a condition that we must meet in order to approach Him in prayer.

If we are to grow in our relationship with God and become strong people of prayer, we must learn to obey. Keeping free from sin is not enough. Neither is faith. If our mouths say that we believe, but our actions don't back up that belief with a strong display of obedience, it shows the weakness of our belief. Obedience should be a natural outgrowth of faith in God. He that obeys God, trusts Him; he that trusts Him, obeys Him.

Norman Vincent Peale told a story from his boyhood that gives insight into the way disobedience hinders our prayers. As a boy, he once got ahold of a big black cigar. He headed into a back alley where he figured no one would see him, and he lit it.

As he smoked it, he discovered that it didn't taste good, but it sure made him feel grown up. As he puffed away, he noticed that a man was walking down the alley in his direction. As the man got closer, Norman realized—to his horror—that it was his father. It was too late to try to throw away the cigar, so he put it behind his back and tried to act as casual as possible.

They greeted each other, and to young Norman's dismay, his father began to chat with him. Desperate to divert his father's attention, the boy spotted a nearby billboard advertising the circus.

"Can I go to the circus, Dad?" he pleaded. "Can I go when it comes to town? *Please,* Dad?"

"Son," his father answered quietly but firmly, "never make a petition while at the same time trying to hide smoldering disobedience behind your back."

Peale never forgot his father's response. And it taught him a valuable lesson about God. He cannot ignore our disobedience even when we try to distract Him. Only our obedience restores our relationship with Him and gives our prayers power.

Prayer Killer #4: Lack of Transparency with God and with Others

On June 4, 1994, I had the privilege of speaking to 65,000 men at Promise Keepers in Indianapolis, Indiana. I spoke on the value of moral integrity, valuing our wives, and keeping ourselves sexually pure. During the weeks leading up to the event, I never in my life felt so much sexual temptation and pressure. I told my wife, Margaret, "Don't let me out of your sight for the next few weeks." I knew I was under serious attack.

I also made a decision at that time to share my struggles with my prayer partners. It wasn't easy, but I reasoned that if I was honest with them, they would be able to pray more effectively for me. My transparency made it possible for them to pray for me very specifically, and I was able to stand against temptation. I believe it was their prayers that helped me endure this incredibly difficult time and remain faithful to God.

James 5:16 says, "Therefore, confess your sins to one another, and pray for one another, so that you may be healed" (NASB). James is sharing a truth about God: When we confess our sins to one another, which requires us to be absolutely transparent, God is able to heal and cleanse us. We experience a spiritual, physical, and emotional restoration. In addition, our transparency helps others, because it shows them that they are not alone in their difficulties.

Dietrich Bonhoeffer has written about the importance of sharing openly with other Christians. In *Life Together,* he says:

> In confession the light of the Gospel breaks into the darkness and seclusion of the heart. The sin must be brought into the light. The unexpressed must be openly spoken and acknowledged. All that is secret and hidden is made manifest. It is a hard struggle until the sin is openly admitted. But God breaks the gates of brass and bars of iron. Our brother breaks the circle of self-deception. A man who confesses his sin in the presence of a brother knows that he is no longer alone with himself. He experiences the presence of God in the reality of the other person.

The most difficult part in being honest is confessing. Ego becomes a stumbling block, as does fear of hurting our image. It's something that our entire society struggles with. Everyone wants to blame others for their shortcomings and problems.

Over the years, I've had to work with my son, Joel Porter, on this issue. He's reluctant to confess when he does something that isn't right. When he was little and he did something wrong, he used to say, "Sorry." Margaret and I had to keep telling him, "Joel, when you do wrong, say 'I am sorry.'" He liked to leave himself out of the equation, and having him apologize for what *he'd* done was the whole point.

Transparency is a difficult thing for a lot of people. Many pastors I know have an especially hard time with it. But openness with others can have a profound effect on you. Transparency with God when you pray puts you on His agenda instead of your own. And it also releases other believers to pray for you strategically and specifically.

Prayer Killer #5: Unforgiveness

You may remember the Scripture passage in which Peter asked Jesus about forgiveness. He asked, "Lord, how many times shall I forgive my brother when he sins against me? Up to seven times?" (Matt. 18:21). Hebrew law required a person to forgive a person three times for an offense. Peter, by suggesting seven, thought he was being very lenient and forgiving. He was probably shocked when he heard Jesus' answer: "Not seven times, but seventy-seven times" (Matt. 18:22).

Jesus was trying to teach Peter that forgiveness is not a matter of mathematics. Nor is it a choice of words. It is an attitude of the heart, and it is the Holy Spirit who empowers us to forgive. Why is forgiveness so important? The answer is found in Matthew 6:14-15, "For if you forgive men when they sin against you, your heavenly Father will also forgive you. But if you do not forgive men their sins, your Father will not forgive your sins."

Forgiving and being forgiven are inseparable twins. When a person refuses to forgive another, he is hurting himself, because his lack of forgiveness can take hold of him and make him bitter. And a person cannot enter prayer with bitterness and come out with blessings. Forgiveness allows your heart to be made not only right, but light.

Prayer Killer #6: Wrong Motives

I once heard a story about a minister who was taking a walk down a row of fine old Victorian homes one day. As he strolled along, he spotted a young boy jumping up and down on the front porch of a beautiful old house. He was trying to reach the old-fashioned doorbell that was set high next to the door, but he was too short.

Feeling sorry for the youngster, the minister went up the walk, stepped up onto the porch, and rang the bell vigorously for him. Then he smiled down at the young lad and said, "And now what, young man?"

"Now," exclaimed the young boy, "we run like crazy!"

The man misjudged the motives of the little boy in the story, but God makes no mistakes about our motives. When they're not right, our prayers have no power. James 4:3 says, "When you ask, you do not receive, because you ask with wrong motives."

Sometimes even knowing our own motives can be difficult. In my experience, I've observed two things that quickly expose wrong motives:

1. A PROJECT GREATER THAN OURSELVES:

Big projects—ones that put us in way over our heads—force us to examine why we are doing them. And that process exposes our motives. Think about someone like Noah. God asked him to build an ark at a time when the earth had never seen rain. It was definitely a project that he couldn't do on his own. When his neighbors came to laugh at him and ridicule him, Noah must have searched himself and examined why he was doing it. And that reminded him of his responsibility to God.

2. PRAYER: When we pray, God speaks to us and shows us our motives. If we are acting out of pride, fear, possessiveness, self-satisfaction, convenience, etc., God will show it to us, if only we are willing to listen. And if we are willing, He will change those motives.

Because I always want to try to keep my motives pure, I ask Bill

Klassen, my personal prayer partner, to keep me accountable. One of the questions he always asked me when I was still the senior pastor at Skyline was, "Are you abusing the power you have in the church?" That kept me honest. And knowing I'd have to face Bill each month and answer that question helped remind me to check my motives continually so that they would be pure and in line with God's desires for me.

Prayer Killer #7: Idols in our Lives

When most people think of idols, they think of statues that are worshiped as gods. But an idol can be anything in our life that comes between us and God. Idols come in many forms: money, career, children, pleasure. Once again, it's an issue of the heart.

Ezekiel 14:3 clearly shows the negative effect of anything that comes between a person and God. It says, "Son of man, these men have set up idols in their hearts and put wicked stumbling blocks before their faces. Should I let them inquire of me at all?" The distaste that God has for idols should be clear from this passage. He doesn't even want an idol worshiper to talk to Him. On the other hand, when we remove idols from our lives, we become ripe for a personal revival.

Take a look at your own life. Is there anything that you're putting ahead of God? Sometimes it's hard to tell. One of the ways to know that something in your life is an idol is to ask yourself, "Would I be willing to give this thing up if God asked me to?" Look honestly at your attitude toward your career, possessions, and family. If there are things you wouldn't release to God, then they're blocking your access to Him

Prayer Killer #8: Disregard for Others

Psalm 33:13 says, "From heaven the LORD looks down and sees all mankind." God's perspective is expansive. He loves everyone, and His desire is that we care for others in the same way. When we disregard others, it grieves Him.

Scripture is full of verses supporting God's desire for unity among all believers—between Christian brothers and sisters, husbands and wives, laypeople and pastors. For example, in John 13·34, Jesus said, "A new command I give you: Love one another. As I have loved you, so you must love one another." First Peter 3:7 exhorts husbands and wives to be considerate to one other. Otherwise, it says, their prayers will be hindered. And 1 Peter 2:13 says, "Submit yourselves for the Lord's sake to every authority instituted among men."

One of the added benefits of prayer is that it helps you learn to love others. It's impossible for a person to hate or criticize someone they're praying for. Prayer breeds compassion, not competition. For example, Bill Klassen often tells people about how he was as a young Christian. He said that after church on most Sundays he'd have "roast pastor" for lunch. He criticized his pastor pretty severely. But as he grew in his prayer life, God began to break his heart for pastors. His spirit of criticism melted into a spirit of compassion. And it ultimately directed him to start his own "Prayer Partner" ministry, devoted to motivating laymen to pray for their pastors. That was quite a turnaround.

Prayer Killer #9: Disregard for God's Sovereignty

I believe very strongly in the sovereignty of God. I think that's one of the things that has helped me remain positive during difficult times over the years. I know that God knows me completely and knows what's best for me. Jeremiah 1:5 says, "Before I formed you in the womb I knew you, before you were born I set you apart."

When Jesus showed the disciples how to pray, the first thing He did was teach them to honor God for who He is, "Our Father in heaven, hallowed be your name, your kingdom come, your will be done on earth as it is in heaven" (Matt. 6:9-10). That is a clear acknowledgment that God is in charge, that He is sovereign. And it establishes our relationship to Him: that of a child under the authority of his Father. Any time we disregard the divine order of things, we're out-of-bounds, and we hinder our relationship with our heavenly Father.

Prayer Killer #10: Unsurrendered Will

There once was a Scottish woman who earned a modest living by peddling her wares along the roads of her country. Each day she would travel about, and when she came to an intersection, she would toss a stick into the air. Whichever way the stick pointed was the way she went. On one occasion an old man stood across the road from her as she tossed the stick into the air once, twice, three times. Finally the old man asked, "Why are you throwing that stick like that?"

"I'm letting God show me which way to go by using this stick,' she said.

"Then why did you throw it three times?" the old man asked.

"Because the first two times, He was pointing me in the wrong direction," was her reply.

The ultimate purpose of prayer is not to get what we want, but to learn to want what God gives. But that will never happen if we don't surrender our will and put ourselves on God's agenda instead of our own.

A person whose will is surrendered to God has a relationship with Him similar to the one described in the parable of the vine and the branches. It says, "If you remain in me and my words remain in you, ask whatever you wish, and it will be given you" (John 15:7). The branch depends on the vine and lives in one accord with it. In return, the vine provides it with everything it needs, and the result is great fruitfulness.

There are great benefits to surrendering your will to God. One is that God promises to answer your prayers and grant your requests. Another is that we get to receive the power of Christ through the Holy Spirit. Just as with the vine and the branches, He flows through us, gives us power, and produces fruit.

Developing an effective prayer life depends on keeping your relationship with God strong and uncluttered by sin and disobedience. First Peter 3:12 says, "The eyes of the Lord are on the righteous and his ears are attentive to their prayer, but the face of the Lord is against those who do evil." If we strive for righteousness and confess our errors, we can remain close to God. But maintaining our relationship with Him is an ongoing process. A Christian can't simply pray once through a list like these ten prayer killers and expect to be done with it. Every day we need to go to God and ask Him to reveal anything that may be hindering our progress.

Look at Psalm 139:23-24. It contains the words of David, a man after God's own heart, who had one of the best relationships with God in all the Bible:

> **Search me, O God, and know my heart;**
> **test me and know my anxious thoughts.**
> **See if there is any offensive way in me,**
> **and lead me in the way everlasting.**

David overcame some horrible sins in his life to be close to God. He was a murderer and adulterer, yet he humbled himself before God and confessed his sins. And that allowed him to come closer to God and keep growing and building in his relationship with Him.

David is a great model for us to follow. If God was able to forgive him and build a special relationship with him, then He can do the same with us. If we are faithful, God will draw us close to Him. And He will answer our prayers.

DISCUSSION QUESTIONS

1. Can you remember a time when someone hung up on you on the telephone? How did it make you feel?

2. What are the similarities between hanging up the phone on someone and harboring one of the prayer killers? How do you think God feels when we "hang up" on Him?

3. Different people struggle with different prayer killers. Of the ten listed in the chapter, which ones are you most susceptible to? Why are these particularly difficult for you?
   a. unconfessed sin
   b. lack of faith
   c. disobedience
   d. lack of transparency with God and others
   e. unforgiveness
   f. wrong motives
   g. idols in my life
   h. disregard for others
   i. disregard for God's sovereignty
   j. unsurrendered will

4. What are some of the benefits of having open communication with God without any spiritual hindrances?

5. What things can you do to prevent yourself from falling into the habit of any of the ten prayer killers?

5

EXPANDING YOUR PRAYER FOCUS

My intercessor is my friend as my eyes pour out tears to God;
on behalf of a man he pleads with God as a man
pleads for his friend.
Job 16:20–21

In the summer of 1876, grasshoppers nearly destroyed the crops in Minnesota. So in the spring of 1877, farmers were worried. They believed that the dreadful plague would once again visit them and again destroy the rich wheat crop, bringing ruin to thousands of people.

The situation was so serious that Governor John S. Pillsbury proclaimed April 26 as a day of prayer and fasting. He urged every man, woman, and child to ask God to prevent the terrible scourge. On that April day all schools, shops, stores, and offices were closed. There was a reverent, quiet hush over all the state.

The next day dawned bright and clear. Temperatures soared to what they ordinarily were in midsummer, which was very peculiar for April. Minnesotans were devastated as they discovered billions of grasshopper larvae wiggling to life. For three days the unusual heat persisted, and the larvae hatched. It appeared that it wouldn't be long before they started feeding and destroying the wheat crop.

On the fourth day, however, the temperature suddenly dropped, and that night frost covered the earth. It killed every one of those creeping, crawling pests as surely as if poison or fire had been used. Grateful farmers never forgot that day. It went down in the history of Minnesota as the day God answered the prayers of the people.

THE POWER OF PRAYING FOR OTHERS

That event in Minnesota over 120 years ago shows what can happen when people are willing to pray, not only for themselves, but for others. That is when prayer really becomes exciting. You can actually see your prayers being answered. You can see lives change, and that's the greatest joy of praying for others.

The act of praying or pleading with God on behalf of someone else is commonly called intercession. It is a selfless act and is considered by some people to be the highest form of prayer. Jesus was an intercessor. During the last hours before He was arrested and crucified, He spent time interceding for the disciples and the believers who would come after them, which includes us! He said:

> **I pray for them. I am not praying for the world, but for those you have given me, for they are yours. . . . Holy Father, protect them by the power of your name—the name you gave me—so that they may be one as we are one. . . . My prayer is not for them alone. I pray also for those who will believe in me through their message, that all of them may be one, Father, just as you are in me and I am in you. (John 17:9-21)**

Jesus came into this world to talk to people about God, but while He was here, He also talked to God about people. And now in heaven, He continues to pray for us, interceding on our behalf (Rom. 8:34).

CHARACTERISTICS OF AN INTERCESSOR

Anyone can intercede for another person. People do it all the time. If you're married, chances are that you pray for your spouse. If you're a parent, you probably pray for your children—all the time—asking God to protect them and help them learn and grow. Those are examples of intercession.

Occasionally I find people whose desire to pray for others is so strong that they are *compelled* to intercede for others. Sometimes they pray primarily for one particular person, but usually they pray for many. Bill Klassen, who started the prayer partner ministry at Skyline, and his wife, Marianne, are two people who feel that way about prayer. I believe they have been *called* to be intercessors. Men and women like them who have that kind of heart for prayer often share three characteristics:

1. IDENTIFICATION: People who feel called to intercede for someone usually have a very strong identification or empathy for that person. Sometimes that identification begins with a respect for that person's ministry or position, such as that of their pastor. But the feelings of connection and empathy almost always deepen on a more personal level.

I mentioned previously that I have a prayer partner named Fred Rowe who prays in his car early in the morning. Fred committed himself to praying for me and the church after coming to a prayer partner breakfast at Skyline. He later told about a prayer time he had where he began to cry uncontrollably and he didn't know why. No matter what he did, he couldn't stop. As he prayed and asked God what was going on, he got the answer. "I'm giving you My heart for John," he felt God telling him. Since then, Fred has been an incredible prayer support who has a strong desire to pray not only for me, but for other pastors as well.

2. SACRIFICE: Intercessors display a willingness to make sacrifices for the people for whom they pray. They often spend lengthy periods of time pleading with God on others' behalf. For example, look at Moses. He interceded on behalf of all the children of Israel after the fiasco of the golden calf. He was willing to sacrifice even his own soul. He said to God, "Please forgive their sin—but if not, then blot me out of the book you have written" (Ex. 32:32). Moses had an enduring relationship with the people of Israel and felt responsible for them. He spent a lot of time interceding on their behalf.

3. AUTHORITY: Willingness to sacrifice is the price of intercession, but with it comes authority with God through the power of the Holy Spirit. God rewards those who are willing to stand in the gap for others and plead for them.

HOW TO PRAY FOR OTHERS

Do you feel *compelled* to intercede for others the way Bill and Marianne Klassen do? If so, that's great. God will honor that desire. But most Christians don't start out with that kind of strong compulsion to intercede. Even Moses went through a forty-year preparation process in the desert before God called him to come to the aid of the Hebrews in Egypt. As far as we know, he didn't become an intercessor until he was eighty years old.

Inside, you probably do have some kind of desire to pray for others (you probably wouldn't be reading this book if you didn't). And that's all you need. You can help others, including your pastor, people in your church, and your family.

If you are ready to pray for others but aren't sure how to go about it, here are four things that you can always pray, whether you're a pastor praying for your people, a layperson praying for a church leader, a citizen praying for government officials, a parent praying for a child, or a believer praying for an unsaved person:

1. Pray that They Know God's Will for Their Lives

The best that people can hope for in life is to know God and fulfill the purpose He has planned for them. So it naturally follows that we should ask God for that when we pray for others.

The apostle Paul, a good leader and strong man of prayer, made it a practice to pray that others would know God's purpose for them, and we can learn a lot from what he says about intercessory prayer. In his letter to the Colossians, Paul wrote, "We have not stopped praying for you and asking God to fill you with the knowledge of his will through all spiritual wisdom and understanding" (1:9). Paul recognized that knowing God's will was a spiritual issue and that prayer was needed for people to know it. For that reason he prayed that the people in the church at Colosse would know God's will, His purpose.

2. Pray That They Would Do God's Will in Their Lives

Paul prayed that the people would know God's will, but he also understood that *knowing* God's will did not guarantee *doing* God's will. So he took his prayers for others one step further. He prayed that they would act on what they learned. The next verse in his letter goes on to say, "We pray this in order that you may live a life worthy of the Lord and may please him in every way: bearing fruit in every good work" (1:10). Only through action does a person fulfill the purpose God has for him.

When you begin praying for purpose in another person's life, it helps to be as specific as possible in your request. We probably won't be able to pray about the details because we won't know exactly what God's will is for their life. But we can be specific about the process. Pray in three areas for them.

- **KNOWLEDGE:** First pray that they would know God's will, that He would communicate it to them with clarity, and that they would understand it.
- **ATTITUDE:** Next, pray that they would have the right attitude toward what God has to tell them. This is often a much more difficult step for people to take. It's one thing to know God's will, but it's another to be willing to change how we feel about it and accept it.
- **BEHAVIOR:** Finally, pray that they would be able to change their behavior to align themselves with God's will. That is often the most difficult step in change because it requires people to face the unknown or do things they're not used to, and that makes them feel uncomfortable. For example, I once mentored a person who had never been an encourager, but who wanted to become more affirming. Every couple of weeks during our mentoring time he'd say, "It just doesn't feel right; I feel so awkward." But I kept praying for him and he kept working at it, and before long, he had learned to encourage others.

When I was growing up, my parents prayed a lot for my brother Larry, my sister Trish, and me—and they still pray for us every day. One of the things I heard them pray most often was that we would know God's will for our lives. I believe those prayers made an incredible difference in us. For example, I've always known what God has wanted me to do. From the time of my earliest memories, beginning when I was about three years old, I knew that I was supposed to be a preacher. I followed that calling, and God has blessed me as a result. But I might not have known it without the prayers of my parents.

3. Pray for Productivity in Their Lives

In Paul's letter to the Colossians, he also prayed that the people would lead productive lives. He wrote, "And we pray this in order that you may live a life worthy of the Lord and may please him in every way: bearing fruit in every good work" (1:10).

The life of an obedient Christian is fruitful. That is how our Creator designed us to be. As Jesus said, "I chose you and appointed you to go and bear fruit—fruit that will last" (John 15:16). The greatest fruit that a person's life can bear has lasting value; usually that means actions with eternal consequences, such as salvation for unbelievers and ministry to other members of the body of Christ. So when you pray for others, pray that they would be productive, and that they would choose to bear fruit that is eternal.

4. Pray for Them to Have a Growing Relationship with God

Paul also prayed that the people would keep "growing in the knowledge of God" (Col. 1:10). He knew that everything in life hinged on the health of our relationship with our Creator. And he had also learned a valuable lesson as a result of the growth in his own relationship with God: contentment (Phil. 4:11-12).

I once read a great definition of happiness. It said, "Happiness is growth." I've found that to be true in my life. When I'm growing in my relationship with God and being obedient to Him, that is when I've been most content. And that's a good thing to ask God to do for others in prayer.

5. Pray for Power in Their Lives

When Paul prayed, he also asked that the people would receive power. He wrote that he wanted them to be "strengthened with all power according to his glorious might so that [they] may have great endurance and patience" (Col. 1:11). The power he was speaking of was that of God's Holy Spirit.

As Christians, each of us can be empowered by the Holy Spirit. If we are to do anything of value, we must have Him as the source of our power. Think of yourself as being similar to a vacuum cleaner in your home. Like us, a vacuum cleaner was created with certain inherent abilities, and it has a specific purpose. But if it's not plugged in and receiving power, it's useless. It depends on another source to make it effective. If you pull the plug, it's worthless.

We're like that. Without the power from our Source, Jesus Christ, we're not effective. We may be able to do some things on our own, but they have no eternal value. When we really understand this, we begin to see ourselves as we really are. We realize that we need and must depend on God.

That's why it's important to ask God to give others His power as we pray for them. Without that power, they won't be able to make a difference for Him. But with that power, they can show strength in the face of adversity, patience during trials, and endurance to finish the race God has laid out before them. And then, in the end, we can hope that God will tell the Christian brothers and sisters we prayed for, "Well done, good and faithful servant."

6. Pray for Them to Have a Right Attitude

Finally, Paul prayed that the people in the church at Colosse would be "joyfully giving thanks to the Father, who has qualified you to share in the inheritance of the saints in the kingdom of light" (1:11-12). In other words, Paul was praying that they would maintain a positive, joyful attitude. You may ask, "Why would Paul pray for people's attitudes?" You can find the answer in this poem that I wrote a decade ago:

WHAT IS YOUR ATTITUDE?

It is the "advance man" of our true selves.
Its roots are inward but its fruit is outward.
It is our best friend or our worst enemy.
It is more honest and more consistent than our words.
It is an outward look based on past experiences.
It is never content until it is expressed.
It is the librarian of our past;
It is the speaker of our present;
It is the prophet of our future.

Our attitude impacts nearly every aspect of our lives. It influences our behavior, affects our ability to learn, determines our contentment, and colors our relationships, including our relationship with God. It affects each person's life and Christian walk greater than you might think.

As you pray for others to keep a joyful attitude, remember that joy is different from happiness. Joy is internal and based on Christ. Happiness is external and based on circumstances. Joy is eternal and linked to our salvation, where happiness is temporary and based on fleeting emotions. Pray that your Christian brothers and sisters find *joy* in their lives, and that as a result, they would be salt and light to those around them.

As you spend an increasing amount of time praying for others, you will find that your attitude toward people improves. It becomes more positive and compassionate. And your prayer time will also mature. You will find that:

- **WHERE YOU ONCE FOCUSED ON RECEIVING, YOUR CONCERN HAS SHIFTED TO GIVING.** "It is more blessed to give than to receive" (Acts 20:35).
- **WHERE YOU WERE ONCE CONCERNED WITH YOUR INJURIES, YOUR FOCUS HAS CHANGED TO HEALING.** "Bear with each other and forgive whatever grievances you may have against one another. Forgive as the Lord forgave you" (Col. 3:13).
- **WHERE YOU ONCE THOUGHT ABOUT YOUR PROBLEMS, YOUR FOCUS IS NOW ON GOD'S POWER.** "Trust in him at all times, O people; pour out your hearts to him, for God is our refuge" (Ps. 62:8).

In *Celebration of Discipline*, Richard Foster said:

> To pray is to change. Prayer is the central avenue God uses to transform us. If we are unwilling to change, we will abandon prayer as a noticeable characteristic of our lives. The closer we come to the heartbeat of God the more we see our need and the more we desire to be conformed to Christ. To pray is to change.

That is true of prayer, but it's also true that prayer changes others.

I mentioned in the previous chapter that at one time my brother, Larry, was not walking with the Lord. Back then he was pursuing his own agenda. He was a businessman and very successful financially. All during the time that he was neglecting his relationship with God, both of my parents interceded for him every day, asking God to bring Larry back to Him.

One afternoon while playing tennis together, I finally asked Larry, "When are you going to stop messing around and come back to God?"

"John," he replied, "I don't know—but I just know I will someday. No matter what I do, I can't get away from the prayers of our parents."

Larry was right. He couldn't get away from their prayers, and after a number of years, he came back to the Lord. By then he had become financially independent. He changed his focus and began using his resources for things of eternal value. Now he's not only a tither and giver to his church, but he's also involved in many organizations dedicated to serving people and growing God's kingdom: He's a trustee at Indiana Wesleyan University. He is the director of the RTN radio network, a system of seven nonprofit Christian radio stations. He's a past director of Health Care Ministries, and the current director of World Gospel Missions—organizations that provide direct support to medical mission programs in Third World countries. And he's also a board member of INJOY, my organization that teaches and equips Christian leaders.

When Larry gets to heaven, I believe God will reward his life of obedience. But I also believe that my dad and mom will share in that reward. Without their faithful prayers, Larry might never have found his way back to God. And the thousands of people whose lives he's touched would have missed out on the blessing God had for them.

DISCUSSION QUESTIONS

1. Why do you think Moses felt compelled to pray for the children of Israel? Did it have anything to do with his relationship to them?

2. Has there been a time in your life when you felt strongly that you should pray for someone close to you—a child, spouse, or friend? Describe that feeling and the circumstances surrounding it.

3. For you, which is the most difficult part of doing God's will?
    a. knowing God's will
    b. having an accepting attitude toward God's will
    c. changing your behavior to obey God's will

4. Describe a time when you tried to perform a ministry task without relying on God for power and strength. What were the results? Did you learn anything from the experience that you could apply to your next attempt?

5. Break into groups of two or three and pray for one other person in each of the areas mentioned in the chapter:
    a. Pray that they know God's will for their lives.
    b. Pray that they would do God's will in their lives.
    c. Pray for productivity in their lives.
    d. Pray for them to have a growing relationship with God.
    e. Pray for power in their lives.
    f. Pray for them to have a right attitude.

6

PROTECTING AND PARTNERING WITH YOUR PASTORS

I urge, then, first of all, that requests, prayers, intercession and thanksgiving be made for everyone—for kings and all those in authority, that we may live peaceful and quiet lives in all godliness and holiness.
1 Timothy 2:1–2

During the last couple of years, Bill Hybels and I have enjoyed partnering together to teach several conferences for pastors. Bill is the senior pastor of Willow Creek Community Church in the Chicago area—a church he started from scratch and that has become one of the largest churches in North America. He is a wonderful brother and a great leader.

Bill and I find teaching and equipping pastors to be an incredibly rewarding experience. We know that for every pastor we help in a conference, we positively touch the lives of hundreds or thousands of people back in their congregations. An important part of those conferences is the time we set aside to pray for the pastors who are attending. We've found that for some of them, the prayer time is transforming.

After a recent conference, I received a letter from one of the pastors who attended. Here's part of what he wrote:

Dear John,

"Even youths grow tired and weary, and young men stumble and fall" (Isa. 40:30). It is amazing how God answers prayer and how He speaks to us. Many people were praying for me yesterday [at the conference]. Some didn't even know me or know why they were praying for me.

I'm a twenty-four-year-old children's pastor at a church in southwest Chicago. Tuesday morning [two days before the conference] I handed my senior pastor and the chairman of the church board my resignation letter. I had resigned out of extreme hurt and sorrow and even out of some anger and bitterness due to a church split which took two-thirds of the core attenders out of our fellowship only one and a half months ago. Since the split, God has been trying to talk with me, but I've been too sad and hurt to be able to hear Him.

Yesterday God had you pray, "God, some here may even have written their resignation letters just before coming to this conference." I almost fell off the front pew! Wow! God couldn't have gotten my attention better if He had hit me over the head with a two-by-four!

That evening I went to my hotel and prayed, journaled, walked, and prayed! God spoke to me. I got on the phone and called the chairman of the board, who had earlier pleaded with me not to send the letter to the rest of the board until after the conference. I called him and gave him the news that I was no longer resigning. He wept like a baby and thanked God. . . .

THE DIFFICULT JOB OF LEADING THE CHURCH

This pastor was saved from leaving his ministry because of the prayer he received. But for every pastor like him who receives help in prayer, there are dozens who are going it alone. I receive about a thousand letters each year from pastors. Many of them are discouraged and ready to quit the ministry. And many times the people in their churches aren't aware of the struggles they're going through.

I've found that most laypeople don't have any idea about the tough time pastors have. Many think pastors have few problems, and they mistakenly believe that people in full-time Christian service have special favor with God that protects them from the ordinary difficulties of life. But nothing could be further from the truth. Pastors experience all the same difficulties you do, plus they have the incredibly demanding job of leading a church.

Bill Hybels said in one of our recent conferences that most laypeople have no idea how difficult it is to run a church. He believes the church is the most leadership-intensive enterprise in society, more difficult than leading in business (which Bill has also done). The work of the church is building and redeeming lives, an intangible process. The workers are all volunteers who can simply leave when disciplined or called to commitment. And each individual life that God calls the leader to reach must be met in a unique way (there's no mass production in the church). Even when recruiting workers, the church leader can't offer monetary incentives or benefits. The best he can do is promise them work without pay, time away from their families, and—if things go according to Scripture— suffering as part of their reward.

THE MYTH OF THE PERFECT PASTOR

Put into this tough environment a person whose people give him very little help but expect him to be a great communicator in the pulpit, an incredible organizer and leader in the office, and a perfect husband and parent at home. That's a heavy burden for anybody to carry.

In his book *Pastors at Risk*, H. B. London quotes some startling statistics from a 1991 survey of pastors conducted by Fuller Institute. Here is what the survey said:

90 percent of pastors work more than forty-six hours a week.

80 percent believe pastoral ministry has affected their families negatively.

33 percent say that being in the ministry is an outright hazard to their family.

75 percent report a significant stress-related crisis at least once in their ministry.

50 percent feel unable to meet the needs of the job.

90 percent feel they were inadequately trained to cope with ministry demands.

70 percent say they have a lower self-image than when they started in the ministry.

40 percent report a serious conflict with a parishioner at least once a month.

33 percent confess having been involved in some inappropriate sexual behavior with someone in the church.

70 percent do not have someone they consider a close friend.

These statistics are heartbreaking. They show how difficult the struggle is for many pastors and how much they need your assistance.

PROBLEMS CHURCH LEADERS FACE

I spent twenty-five years as a senior pastor in local churches. Now I spend time with thousands of pastors and church leaders from over forty denominations each year, so I know what they struggle with. Let me give you the top five difficulties pastors face today:

1. Loneliness

The statistic showing that 70 percent of all pastors don't have a close friend really says a lot about how lonely pastors get. That loneliness comes to some pastors because they don't want the people to know how difficult things are. They are reluctant to be transparent and vulnerable because they think they're supposed to have all the answers. Another reason for loneliness is that leadership naturally tends to isolate leaders from other people. As I often tell people in seminars, "It's lonely at the top, so you'd better know why you're there."

2. Stress

Church leaders are highly susceptible to stress. All their work has eternal consequences, and that can be a heavy burden. They are also highly visible. They and their families live in a fishbowl, subject to comments and criticisms from everyone who sees them. As my friend Peter Wagner says in *Prayer Shield,* "The pastor is closely observed, and it's no secret that just knowing this places a difficult burden on pastors. They need supernatural help to handle that situation well."

About twenty years ago, a funny piece circulated among church leaders. It's called "The Perfect Pastor." I don't know who wrote it, but it's a wonderful composite of the expectations that every pastor feels from his people:

> After hundreds of years the perfect pastor's been found. He is the church elder who'll please everyone. He preaches exactly twenty minutes and then sits down. He condemns sin, but never steps on anybody's toes.
>
> He works from eight in the morning to ten at night, doing everything from preaching sermons to sweeping. He makes $400 per week, gives $100 a week to the church, drives a late-model car, buys lots of books, wears fine clothes, and has a nice family. He always stands ready to contribute to every other good cause, too, and to help panhandlers who drop by the church on their way to somewhere.

He is thirty-six years old, and has been preaching forty years. He is tall, on the short side; heavyset, in a thin sort of way; and handsome. He has eyes of blue or brown (to fit the occasion), and wears his hair parted in the middle—left side dark and straight, right side brown and wavy.

He has a burning desire to work with the youth, and spends all his time with the senior citizens. He smiles all the time while keeping a straight face, because he has a keen sense of humor that finds him seriously dedicated. He makes fifteen calls a day on church members, spends all his time evangelizing nonmembers, and is always found in his study if he is needed. Unfortunately he burnt himself out and died at the age of thirty-two.

Because so many pastors genuinely love people and want to help them, they get pulled in too many directions—and that causes stress.

3. Feelings of Inadequacy

As the statistic in the Fuller Institute survey said, nine out of ten pastors experience feelings of inadequacy because they don't feel as though they've been equipped for the job they do. I would guess that you would be hard-pressed to find another profession where that statistic is so high. Further intensifying those feelings is the fact that some pastors' families feel uncomfortable with their position in the church. My friend H. B. London, who ministers to pastors all across the country, recently told me that at one time, 40 percent of the letters he received weren't from pastors, but from their wives. They were very angry with God, the church, the people, and their husbands because of their situations. When family members feel this kind of resentment, they're not likely to be very supportive, and that only adds to the existing feelings of inadequacy.

4. Depression

The pressures of leadership—along with loneliness, stress, and feelings of inadequacy—can push leaders into depression. I recently did a study of Elijah, a great man of God in the Old Testament. Even he got depressed. In 1 Kings 19:4, it says that following his experience on Mount Carmel, "He himself went a day's journey into the desert. He came to a broom tree, sat down under it and prayed that he might die. 'I have had enough, LORD,' he said. 'Take my life; I am no better than my ancestors.'" Elijah had been obedient to God—calling fire down from heaven to show God's power, putting to death all the false prophets of Baal, and praying for the lengthy drought to end—yet he still felt like giving up. So it should be no surprise when the same thing happens to today's church leaders.

5. Spiritual Warfare

Early in my ministry, I was naive about how much Christian leaders have to battle the devil. But as I continue in my ministry, I find that I have to fight Satan more and more, and the battles usually occur when I'm making major decisions. I believe the evil one watches for the right time to attack Christian leaders, and he is especially active before an advance for God's kingdom, after a victory, and when a leader is just plain tired.

Jesus' temptation in the wilderness is an excellent example of Satan's desire to attack believers during times of weakness. Jesus went without food during forty days in the desert following His baptism in the Jordan, and Satan saw this as a great opportunity to try to tempt Him. We know this is the way the enemy thought because in Luke 4:13 it says, "When the devil had finished all this tempting, he left him until an *opportune time*" (emphasis added).

Any time a person is doing positive things for God, Satan will try to stop it. The higher you go up the ladder of Christian leadership, the higher you go on Satan's hit list. That means pastors and other church leaders are going to be under continuous spiritual attack because they spend the majority of their time working to build God's kingdom.

PRAYER IS THE ANSWER

Where does a church leader find help to combat all of these difficulties? The answer is prayer. It has the power to overcome any problem or obstacle. Jesus demonstrated this time after time. His prayer in the Garden of Gethsemane just before His death especially emphasized the power of prayer. He said, "Again, I tell you that if two of you on earth agree about anything you ask for, it will be done for you by my Father in heaven. For where two or three come together in my name, there am I with them" (Matt. 18:19-20).

The idea of partnership in prayer is not new. Many times in the New Testament, Christian leaders asked the people to pray for themselves and for others. Paul, for example, asked for prayer from the Romans (15:31), the Ephesians (6:19-20), the Colossians (4:3), and others to whom he wrote. But partnering in prayer goes farther back than that. The first biblical example of prayer partnership can be found in the Old Testament, in Exodus 17:8-13. When the Amalekites attacked the children of Israel, two men—Aaron and Hur—stood with Moses, their leader, and partnered with him by praying for him and supporting him. The Scripture says:

> The Amalekites came and attacked the Israelites at Rephidim. Moses said to Joshua, "Choose some of our men and go out to fight the Amalekites. Tomorrow I will stand on top of the hill with the staff of God in my hands."
> So Joshua fought the Amalekites as Moses had ordered, and Moses, Aaron and Hur went to the top of the hill. As long as Moses held up his hands, the Israelites were win-

ning, but whenever he lowered his hands, the Amalekites were winning. When Moses' hands grew tired, they took a stone and put it under him and he sat on it. Aaron and Hur held his hands up—one on one side, one on the other—so that his hands remained steady till sunset. So Joshua overcame the Amalekite army with the sword.

With the help of Moses' brother Aaron and a layman named Hur, Joshua was able to be victorious against the forces that were trying to destroy God's children.

CHRISTIAN LEADERS CAN'T DO IT ALONE

Moses was one of the greatest leaders who ever lived. He spoke to God face-to-face, as a person would speak to a friend (Ex. 33:11). Yet he still could not do it alone. Even he needed assistance and encouragement. Fortunately, Aaron and Hur recognized his need and helped him. My hope is that you will recognize your church leader's need and come alongside to support him in prayer.

Ministry is never a one-man show; it requires teamwork. However, Americans tend to admire rugged individualists more than team players. We marvel at the way a basketball player like Michael Jordan scores points, yet we overlook the importance of how he works with his teammates. We admire the characters played by John Wayne, or Rambo as portrayed by Sylvester Stallone—lone warriors who can take whatever the enemy can dish out. Radio journalist Paul Harvey once said:

> We have always tended to revere the airplane pilot who did it alone and the country doctor who never left the bedside. Such a spirit of independence served us well and caused us all to grow tall. But we'd never have made it to the moon without a spirit of

interdependence. And we'd never have eradicated typhoid and smallpox and polio without cooperative effort. We've found that no person alone can fetch oil from beneath an ocean. We've found that we are becoming increasingly interdependent—not only in our country, but also all around the world. The spirit of interdependence will not cost more than it is worth. On the steep slope ahead, holding hands is necessary. And it just might be we can learn to enjoy it.

The need for teamwork and cooperation is becoming evident even to everyone. It should be even more obvious to us believers.

In *Prayer Shield,* C. Peter Wagner wrote, "I'm personally convinced that the following statement is true: 'The most under-utilized source of spiritual power in our churches today is intercession for Christian leaders.'"

Aaron and Hur were committed and aggressive prayer partners, ready to jump in and help their leader be all that God intended him to be.

- **THEY SAW THE NEED.**
- **THEY SEIZED THE MOMENT.**
- **THEY SHARED IN THE VICTORY.**

And that's the same kind of assistance church leaders need today. The greatest support anyone can give a leader is to pray for him or her.

HOW TO PRAY FOR YOUR LEADER

At this point, you're probably ready to pray for your pastor, but you may not know how to get started. Pastors and other Christian leaders need prayer in all the same areas you do. But they also have other prayer needs. Several years ago, I saw a prayer guide written by a pastor named Will Bruce entitled, "Pastors Need Prayer, Too."

I thought it had some excellent guidelines, and I gave copies to all of my prayer partners that year. It broke down a leader's prayer needs into four areas. Here are some suggested areas to pray for, taken from his list and modified for your use:

Personal Needs

- **HUMILITY:** Ask God to give your leader true humility, which includes having a servant's heart, being teachable, admitting wrongdoing, being willing to receive positive criticism, and reliance on God.
- **WISDOM TO KNOW GOD'S AGENDA:** Effective leaders function according to God's agenda, not their own. Pray that your leader remains sensitive to God's leading, and that he will live and work according to God's priorities.
- **POSITIVE RELATIONSHIPS:** Ask God to help your leader be patient with himself and others, to interact positively with difficult people in the congregation, and to treat everyone with love and respect.
- **THE FRUIT OF THE SPIRIT:** Every Christian should seek to live a Spirit-filled life. Pray that your leader would have love, joy, peace, patience, kindness, goodness, faithfulness, gentleness, and self-control.
- **HEALTH:** Ask God to give your leader good health and safety when he or she travels.

Family Needs

- **THE PRIORITY OF FAMILY:** The demands of ministry can severely damage a Christian leader's family life. Pray that your church leader would make family his top priority, second only to his relationship with God. Pray that he would spend enough time with them, and minister to their needs first. If your leader has children, pray that they would love God with all their hearts.

- **PROVISION FOR THE FAMILY:** Ask God to meet the needs of your leader and to show the lay leadership in the church how they can better provide for them.

Spiritual Needs

- **TIME ALONE WITH GOD:** Ask God to make prayer, Scripture reading, and worship daily priorities in your leader's life.
- **ANOINTING:** Without the power of the Holy Spirit, a leader can do nothing of value.
- **INTEGRITY:** Your leader struggles with temptation just like any other person. In fact, the enemy will try to tempt him more than others. Satan knows that when he hurts the leader, the followers suffer.
- **PROTECTION FROM SPIRITUAL WARFARE:** Pray that your leader would put on the full armor of God, as outlined in Ephesians 6:10-18, and that he will be given protection from the lust of the flesh, the lust of the eyes, and the pride of life (1 John 2:16).
- **ACCOUNTABILITY:** Ask God to bring into your leader's life other Christian leaders who can keep him accountable.

Congregational Needs

- **EVANGELISM:** Pray that your leader will have a heart for the lost and that he will make evangelism a priority.
- **PERSONAL GROWTH:** A pastor who continues to grow in his spiritual life and his ability to lead is being equipped to help his people grow and develop.

- **MOBILIZATION OF THE LAITY:** Ask God to make your leader an effective motivator and equipper of the people to do the work of the ministry.
- **INTERCESSION:** Pray that your leader would make intercession for the people a daily priority.

WHERE THE LEADER GOES, THE PEOPLE FOLLOW

James 3:1 says, "Not many of you should presume to be teachers, my brothers, because you know that we who teach will be judged more strictly." I believe God will judge leaders by a higher standard because what they do affects so many other people. For example, when I was in high school, I knew a pastor who led a growing, vital church. But then he fell morally. Almost thirty years later, that church still has not recovered. Because of his failure, the church lost its effectiveness.

I want to encourage you to pray for your pastors and church leaders. In doing so, you will be partnering with them in the ministry and giving them protection and empowerment. With your help, they will be able to go places they otherwise could not have gone and do things they never would have been able to do alone. And when they succeed, so do their people. That was the case with Moses during the battle with the Amalekites, and that can be the case for your leader and you.

Never underestimate the power of prayer for a church leader. Let me share with you another letter I received recently. This one came from Pastor Roland Schutz after a leadership conference:

> Last year I went to the Atlanta leadership conference needing a fresh start in ministry. In the previous four years, I had gone through the battle of facing my oldest son's cancer, which by all indications is cured, to grieving the death of my leading layman, and watching

cancer take my secretary of nine years. In that time, the earlier growth God had given my church stopped. I was so discouraged and depressed that I knew I needed a new start. That conference in Atlanta breathed new life into me and my vision of ministry. At age forty-four, I felt like I had been reborn.

The Lord provided me with five prayer partners, and through the year, a vision of what He wants me to do in my ministry. He is calling me to pastor a church of 1,000 people who are ministers, not just attenders. He is giving me success in mentoring other pastors, and I believe 100 pastors will be influenced in that process. He will also use me to influence the planting of ten new churches. . . .

If you begin praying for your leaders today, there's no telling what may happen in your church tomorrow.

DISCUSSION QUESTIONS

1. When you were a kid, who used to stand up for you?

2. If you were a church leader, which of the five common problems that pastors face do you think would affect you the most? Why?
    a. loneliness
    b. stress
    c. feelings of inadequacy
    d. depression
    e. spiritual warfare

3. Have you ever fallen into the trap of thinking your pastor should be perfect? Explain. How does this hurt him?

4. What's the difference between praying for your leader according to your agenda and praying for him or her according to God's agenda?

5. How can you "hold up the hands" of your pastors in prayer, as Aaron and Hur did for Moses? Break into groups of two or three to pray for your leaders.

7

PRAYING YOUR CHURCH TO ITS POTENTIAL

My prayer is not for them alone. I pray also
for those who will believe in me through their message,
that all of them may be one.
John 17:20–21

Several years ago, I read a story recounted by A. M. Hills in *Pentecostal Light*. Here's what he wrote:

> Dr. Wilbur Chapman often told of his experience when he went to Philadelphia to become a pastor of Wanamaker's church. After his first sermon, an old gentleman met him in front of the pulpit and said, "You are pretty young to be pastor of this great church. We have always had older pastors. I am afraid you won't succeed. But you preach the gospel, and I'm going to help you all I can."
>
> "I looked at him," said Dr. Chapman, "and said to myself, 'Here's a crank.'"
>
> But the old gentleman continued: "I am going to pray for you that you may have the Holy Spirit's power upon you, and two others have covenanted to join with me."
>
> Then Dr. Chapman related the outcome. "I did not feel so bad when I learned that he was going to pray for me. The three became ten, the ten became twenty, and the twenty became fifty, and the fifty

became two hundred, who met before every service to pray that the Holy Spirit might come upon me. In another room the eighteen elders knelt so close around me to pray for me that I could put out my hand and touch them on all sides. I always went into my pulpit feeling that I would have the anointing in answer to the prayers of the 219 men.

"It was easy to preach, a real joy. Anybody could preach with such conditions. And what was the result? We received 1,100 into our church by conversion in three years, 600 of which were men. It was the fruit of the Holy Spirit in answer to the prayers of those men. I do not see how the average pastor, under average circumstances preaches at all.

"Church members have much more to do than go to church as curious, idle spectators to be amused and entertained. It is their business to pray mightily that the Holy Ghost will clothe the preacher with power and make his words like dynamite."

What an incredible impact a church can make when its people pray! That is what made the difference during the years I was the pastor at Skyline Church. It made the services powerful, it caused me to receive an anointing, and it enabled the church to give and receive incredible blessings.

Have you thought much about the potential of your church? What could it accomplish if it were to reach its potential? How many lives would be transformed? How many lost people would come to Christ? What would be its impact? Paul said God's intention is to use the church to show His wisdom to everyone in heaven and on earth according to His purpose (Eph. 3:9-11). How is your church taking part in that design?

THE POTENTIAL TO REACH THE WORLD

There is nothing in this world that has as much potential to be an instrument of change as the church. Theologian and teacher Dr. Paul Tillich once said:

The church is potentially a powerful body with a necessary arsenal at its disposal to change the moral character of this world. The fact that it is not doing so causes us to be painfully aware that its potential is not being realized. That which is possible is not being produced, for while possessing the dynamite of the Gospel, the church has lost its detonator (explosiveness). As a result of this inaction, the church that the world sees is weak, timid, divided, and crawling instead of flying. While it has material resources to convert the world, it is restricted by its stinginess and narrowness of vision.

The "detonator" that churches lack today is prayer. It has the power to ignite the dynamite of the gospel and powerfully shake the world!

WHAT JESUS WANTS FOR THE CHURCH

Jesus challenges the church with a clear directive for shaking and changing the world when He gave the Great Commission: "Go and make disciples of all nations, baptizing them in the name of the Father and of the Son and of the Holy Spirit, and teaching them to obey everything I have commanded you" (Matt. 28:19-20). But even before He did that, He prayed a special prayer for all believers, which includes us who today make up His church. In the hours before His crucifixion, He prayed the following:

I pray for them [the disciples]. I am not praying for the world, but for those you have given me, for they are yours. . . .

I am coming to you now, but I say these things while I am still in the world, so that they may have the full measure of my joy within them. I have given them your word and

the world has hated them. . . . Sanctify them by the truth;
your word is truth. As you sent me into the world, I have
sent them into the world. . . .

My prayer is not for them alone. I pray also for those
who will believe in me through their message [that's us!],
that all of them may be one, Father, just as you are in me
and I am in you. May they also be in us so that the world
may believe that you have sent me. I have given them the
glory that you gave me, that they may be one as we are one:
I in them and you in me. May they be brought to complete
unity to let the world know that you sent me and have loved
them even as you have loved me.

Father, I want those you have given me to be with me
where I am, and to see my glory, the glory you have given
me because you loved me before the creation of the world
(John 17:9-24).

Jesus' prayer for the church is an excellent model for us to follow
when we pray for the church. He spoke with confidence, knowing
His time had come, but secure in the knowledge that what He began
on earth would be continued through His body of believers—the
church. What He desired for the church can be summarized as five
prayer requests:

1. That People Would Sense the Glory of God

Jesus said, "I have given them the glory that you gave me" (John
17:22). The word *glory* in the Greek comes from the word *doxa*
meaning the visible manifestation of the splendor, power, and
radiance of God. So when Jesus prays these words, His desire is that
His people continually feel and sense the splendor, power, and
radiance of God in their midst.

Whenever God's presence comes down within the church, it lifts
up the people spiritually. And that's when great things begin to

happen. For example, I rededicated my life to Christ and answered the call to preach at age seventeen during a seven-week revival at our church in Circleville, Ohio. The revival wasn't something that had been planned—it just happened because God came. While I was worshiping, I saw the joy and glory of the Lord in my parents' faces and I felt drawn to God in a way I had never felt before. I just *had* to give my life to Him.

Howard Hendricks once said, "The church doesn't need more workers; it needs more worshipers!" True worship is incredible; it's the highest experience possible for Christians. Too many Christians arrive at worship services preoccupied by their problems or focused on what they can *get* from the service instead of what they can *give* to it. But when the people focus on God and give Him glory, He comes and makes the church a place of power. When a church really worships, when its people really seek to please God and have fellowship with Him and other believers, it draws nonbelievers like a magnet. In such a church, the glory of God is revealed.

The real value of any church is not in the facility, the pastor, or the programs. It's not even the people. Churches have value because Jesus is in them. He brings beauty and power with His presence.

2. That We Would Follow the Word of God

Jesus also prayed that we would become followers of the Word of God. He said, "For I gave them the words you gave me and they accepted them" (John 17:8). When the disciples received the words of Jesus, it gave their lives meaning, motivation, and a mission. That's what Jesus desired for His disciples then, and that's what He desires for us today.

When the people in a church are continually studying and learning Scripture, they begin to change. As they realize that the Bible is eternal, relevant, and full of vitality, their lives take on new meaning. Their values change. And they become motivated to grow, change, and become obedient to God and His purpose for the church.

I had a wonderful experience that illustrates the power of following God's Word while I was in my second pastorate in Lancaster, Ohio. Ours was a growing church, and I could see that we would be quickly running out of room. When that happens, a church has three choices: relocate, expand the facilities, or stop growing. We decided to expand.

We immediately began buying property all around the church, but there was one property owner who was determined not to sell. His name was Mr. Shoup. No matter what we said or did, he said he wasn't going to give up his land.

At that time, I was studying the book of Joshua, and when I read a promise the Lord gave Joshua, it struck a chord in me. It said, "Every place on which the sole of your foot treads, I have given it to you" (Josh. 1:3 NASB).

One night about midnight, I couldn't fall asleep, and that verse kept running through my head. So I got up, grabbed my Bible, and told my wife, Margaret, "I'll be back in about an hour." She looked at me and saw that I was barefoot.

"Where are you going?" she asked, bleary-eyed.

"I'm going to claim Joshua's promise over Mr. Shoup's land," I answered and left. That night I tiptoed all around Mr. Shoup's property. It was a cold night, and the dogs were howling. I half expected the police to show up any time. I wondered how I would try to explain what I was doing, prowling around the neighborhood in the middle of the night—barefoot—with a Bible. They would have thought I was nuts.

But God delivered on His promise. We continued to pray, and a couple of months later, Mr. Shoup gave his heart to the Lord and sold us his property. As a result, we were able to expand the church and its ministry. Isaiah 55:11 says, "My word that goes out from my mouth: It will not return to me empty, but will accomplish what

I desire and achieve the purpose for which I sent it." That is always true. We may not always personally see the results of God's Word, but it always achieves its purpose.

3. That We Would Be United in the Love of God

Jesus prayed for all believers to be unified through love. That's because spirit-filled Christians, united in love and guided by a purpose they truly believe in, *can do anything*. They can shake the very gates of hell. But churches are nearly powerless when they aren't unified. They can't take care of their own people, and they can't be an effective witness to people in the community.

Promise Keepers has been an incredible instrument of God for promoting unity, both within the local church and among churches of every denomination. As a result men have been supporting and praying for their pastors and churches, bridges have been built between denominations, and racial and cultural barriers are slowly being broken down.

On February 13-15, 1996, I had the privilege of speaking at the first Promise Keepers Clergy Conference for Men in Atlanta, Georgia. Over 42,000 pastors from nearly every denomination and culture came from around the country to meet together in the Georgia Dome. It was the greatest movement of God I've ever witnessed in my life. It was a joy to hear the worship leader sing, "Do you believe that Jesus Christ is Lord of Lords, and King of Kings," and then to hear 42,000 pastors respond by singing, "Yes, we all agree." My friend Max Lucado, a gifted author and pastor, preached what will probably be remembered as the sermon of the century, calling for unity among churches. The whole experience was a glimpse of what our world could be like if only we were truly united through the love of God.

4. That We Would Go Forth in the Mission of God

Jesus asked that God "sanctify" us so that we would be prepared to go out into the world, just as the apostles were (John 17:17-18). The word *sanctify* means to be set apart and equipped for a special mission. And that mission is to bring the good news to the lost so that they might be saved. Any church that has lost sight of that mission might someday hear words similar to those given by God in Revelation to the church at Ephesus: "Yet I hold this against you: You have forsaken your first love" (2:4).

I must admit, I didn't always give evangelism the time and atten-tion it deserved in my ministry. When I arrived at my first pastorate in Hilham, Indiana, my goal was to build a big church. I started with only three people, but as I rolled up my sleeves, worked hard, and got to know the people of the town, the church began to grow.

One day, Betty, a member of the church, called and asked if I would visit her friend in the hospital, so I did. I visited Bob many times, and we'd talk about all kinds of things. Our favorite subject was the Boston Celtics, our favorite basketball team. One day after I'd visited him and several other people in the hospital, I called home before driving to the office. Margaret was very quiet on the phone, and I asked, "What's the matter, Babe?"

"I just got off the phone with Betty," she said. "Bob died."

"What?" I said. "I was just with him forty-five minutes ago!"

"I know, honey, but he's gone," Margaret said. Her words hung in the air like the ringing of an iron door slamming shut. "Betty wanted to know if you'd do the funeral."

"Sure," I said absentmindedly. "Tell her I'll do it." I was devastated. I realized at that moment that Bob had gone to hell because he had the misfortune of having me as the pastor who visited with him. During our talks, never once had I talked to him about salvation.

"Cancel tonight's service," I told Margaret. "I can't face all those people. I need some time alone."

I did perform Bob's funeral. When I saw the coffin with him in it, I was crushed. I cried, not just because I was grieving Bob's death, but because I had failed to share the gospel with him. It was then that I began wrestling with God. Over the course of the next few months, He began changing my heart. I realized that my agenda was not God's agenda. Finally, one night I got on my knees and gave it over to God in prayer. I gave up my desire to be a great preacher and to grow an impressive church, and I asked God for the power of the Holy Spirit to be a witness, to be a soul-winner for Christ.

And God honored that prayer. I learned to share my faith and become a personal soul-winner. After that, not a week went by that someone in that community didn't get saved. One year I committed to the people in the congregation that I would try to personally lead two hundred people to Christ outside of church. I missed that goal by twelve people, but I learned a lot about soul-winning.

Then I began equipping others to share their faith. At my second church in Lancaster, Ohio, I trained and equipped eighteen soul-winners who were on fire for Jesus. They were responsible for winning over 1,800 people to Christ during the eight years I was in that church. We received a lot of blessings from God there, because I believe the church was doing everything it could to achieve the mission God had given it.

5. That We Would Experience the Joy of God

Jesus said that He wants us to have His full measure of joy (John 17:13). What gives a body of believers joy? Obedience to God in the things Jesus talked about gives joy: giving God glory, following His Word, being united in love, and carrying out His mission.

Adoniram Judson, a nineteenth-century missionary, was known for his joy in the Lord. He went to Burma as a missionary in 1812, filled with God's Spirit and a great desire to preach the gospel It's said that soon after he arrived, he approached a Burmese man, and not knowing the language, simply embraced him. The man went home and reported to his family that he had seen an angel. The joy of Christ was so radiant in Judson's countenance that men called him "Mr. Glory-Face." That's the kind of joy God wants us to experience—and to exhibit to others.

HOW CAN I PRAY FOR THE CHURCH?

You can transform your church and help it reach its potential through prayer. My prayer partners have done it with me, and you can do it too. Here are some ways for you to get started:

1. Pray Continually

Paul's advice to the church in Thessalonica is also good advice for us today. He said, "Be joyful always; pray continually; give thanks in all circumstances, for this is God's will for you in Christ Jesus" (1 Thess. 5:16-18). If we want the church to reach its potential and accomplish its purpose, we need to pray for it all the time.

Over the years, the people who've prayed for me and the church have come up with some creative ways to remind themselves to pray continually. One prayer partner used to set his alarm to go off every hour one day (and night) a month. And another prayer partner, Mike Mullert, used to put a quarter his shoe. Every time he felt it, he'd pray for the church and me. There's really no limit to the things you can do to remind yourself to pray.

2. Pray Strategically

Begin praying for the people and activities of the church. Pray for anointing for the pastor, for people to come to Christ at each service, for newcomers to be drawn to special events, for relationships to grow, for power as people pray at Wednesday night prayer meeting, for children to be saved in Sunday school. Be aware of all the events and activities occurring in your church, then pray for them to succeed.

3. Pray Geographically

I believe there is great value in physically moving to the places where ministry takes place in the church and praying for the people who will be ministered to there. When I was still in the pastorate, some days I used to walk around the church, asking the Lord to just cover each area. For example, many times I went into the nursery and spent some time laying hands on the cribs and baby beds, praying for God to raise up some giants for the kingdom from the children in the church. Maybe the next Billy Graham would be playing in one of those cribs the next week. And each Sunday before the services, my prayer partners used to lay their hands on all the pews in the church, asking God to do something special for the people who would be sitting there that day.

God honors our prayers whether or not we pray geographically. But I think it helps us when we do because we gain a better understanding of what to pray for and how to pray.

4. Pray Powerfully

If you want to pray effectively for your church, pray with power. There are two ways to do that. First, be filled with the Holy Spirit so that you have the power of God within you. Second, pray according to God's Word. When you pray for the church, use Jesus' prayer as the model and pray for the following:

PRAY FOR BELIEVERS TO EXPERIENCE TRUE WORSHIP.

- Pray for an outpouring of God's glory in His church as people acknowledge Him, not only with their lips but with their lives.
- Ask God for a spirit of worship to manifest itself in your church.
- Pray for revival in the churches across our nation and the world.

PRAY THAT BELIEVERS WILL KNOW, ACCEPT, AND OBEY THE WORD OF GOD.

- Pray that God's Word be preached continually in the church.
- Pray for spiritual understanding and discernment among the people.
- Ask God to make the people obedient to His Word.

PRAY FOR UNITY IN THE CHURCH.

- Pray for humility among the church's leaders and body of believers.
- Pray that a spirit of humility and repentance will rise up among all believers.
- Ask God to break down all racial, cultural, and denominational walls.

PRAY FOR SOULS TO BE WON TO CHRIST.

- Ask God to give your church leaders a vision for reaching the lost.
- Pray for workers for the harvest—for believers who will consistently share their faith.
- Pray that local churches across the country would reach out to the lost in their communities.

PRAY FOR JOY IN THE HEARTS AND LIVES OF BELIEVERS.

- Ask God to reveal your church's potential to your leaders and the people.
- Ask God to bring joy to your leaders and the people of the church.

When you begin praying for your church, awesome things will start to happen. Let me tell you the story of a friend of mine, a layman named Doug Bennett who lives in Michigan. In 1987, Doug and his pastor attended a conference where I spoke called "Breaking the 200 Barrier." One of the things I talked about was the prayer partner ministry at Skyline and how it was responsible for the successes that we had experienced.

I didn't know Doug back then, but he later told me that he left that seminar convicted. He felt called to intercede for his pastor and the church, and he committed to praying for their little church of sixty for an hour every Sunday before the service began.

Doug was incredibly excited about praying, but his enthusiasm fell on deaf ears. When he approached his pastor about becoming his personal prayer partner, the pastor wasn't interested. When Doug's fellow board members found out about his prayer time, their response was, "That's nice. Just don't expect us to come to church early to pray." Doug refused to be discouraged; he continued praying. When his old pastor left the church, and a new one took his place, Doug received renewed hope. But when asked about starting a prayer partner ministry, the new pastor said, "We have a prayer meeting on Wednesday nights, and five or six people always come. That's enough."

So Doug continued praying alone. From May 1987 to July 1991, he went to the sanctuary alone every Sunday and prayed for his church and pastor. He had hung on for a long time, but he finally began to have doubts.

"God," he asked while praying one Sunday morning, "can one person really make a difference? Or am I just the biggest fool in this place?" He struggled with that question for two weeks. And finally, God gave him an answer. It was time to move on to another church, but Doug didn't know where.

Doug and his wife, Sherry, left their old church on good terms, and began searching for the new place where God was sending them. A few months later they found it, and in January of 1992, they became members. That's when Doug began asking God what his role would be in this new setting. Very clearly, he got the word: He was to intercede for this pastor and his church. He was to be this pastor's "Bill Klassen"—his personal prayer partner and intercessor.

Doug immediately made an appointment with his pastor, Bill Rudd. When they met, Doug told him, "Pastor, I know you don't really know me. But God brought me here to be your personal intercessor and to surround you with prayer partners."

Bill Rudd's eyes got big, and Doug could see that he almost fell out of his chair. "Wait right here," he said. He got up hurriedly and retrieved something from a nearby file cabinet. "This is last year's annual report. I just wrote it in December. Take a look at this entry on page three," he said. Doug looked at what he had written as one of his goals for 1992. It said, "I am asking God to recruit a band of 'PASTOR'S PRAYER PARTNERS.'"

Then it was Doug's turn to nearly fall out of his chair. For four years God had been preparing and equipping him to come to this pastor's aid.

For the next seven months, the two of them met weekly to pray together. Doug interceded for Bill, and he also started praying for God to bring them forty-eight prayer partners. Then in September of that year, they held a one-day retreat to get a prayer partner ministry going. Seventy-five men showed up at that retreat, and when the retreat was over, they asked for the men who were interested to sign a commitment card to pray for Bill and the church for the coming year. When Doug counted the responses, there were exactly forty-eight.

That was the year their church turned around. Before they started their prayer partner ministry, their church had plateaued at about five hundred people. But as soon as their prayer partners began praying, the church started growing. In the next three and a half years, the church tripled in size, from five hundred to about fifteen hundred. In addition, the church is now in a better position financially than at any other time in its eighty-year history. Lay ministry has also grown and strengthened.

Doug and Bill attribute all the positive changes they've experienced in their church to prayer. And other churches, seeing and hearing about their success, have asked Doug and Bill to help them start prayer partner ministries. So far, they've helped over one hundred churches!

Doug Bennett's prayers are being answered. And as a result, his church has been blessed. Every day it is growing toward its potential. And the same thing can happen in your church. When you start praying, God begins moving. And miracles can happen when you get a whole team of people praying. How to do that is the subject of the next chapter.

DISCUSSION QUESTIONS

1. Have you ever experienced or heard of a story similar to the one about Doug Bennett, where someone prayed for the church and then had the privilege of seeing the prayer answered? Describe what happened.

2. Of the things Jesus prayed for the church, which would you most enjoy seeing come to fruition? Why?
   Seeing the people of the church . . .
   a. sense the glory of God.
   b. follow the Word of God.
   c. become united in the love of God.
   d. go forth in the mission of God.
   e. experience the joy of God.

3. What things might happen if your church reached its potential? Describe them.

4. Name some ways you could pray strategically or geographically for your church.

5. What area of your church is God calling you to pray for? Break into small groups and pray together for your church.

8

ORGANIZING A PRAYER PARTNER TEAM

For where two or three come together in my name,
there am I with them.
Matthew 18:20

Arthur J. Moore was a Methodist bishop early this century. But before he served in that post, he pastored some of the largest Methodist churches in the South. He was a consistent and successful evangelist, and at least one person was converted every Sunday that he preached.

One day just before a worship service, a friend visited Moore and asked him, "How is it that you're so successful?"

"Come with me," Moore said. He took the visitor to the basement, where a prayer meeting was in progress. There were seventy men praying fervently for him and the worship service that was about to begin.

When the prayer partners were finished, they quietly walked up the stairs into the service. Moore turned to his friend and said, "Notice where they sit."

"What do you mean?" he asked Moore, watching them scatter over the sanctuary.

"See," said Moore. "Where each one of them sits down, he is

such a center of divine warmth that anyone frozen in sin who sits near him is liable to thaw out before the service is over."

When a group of people lifts up their church and partners with their leader in prayer, incredible things happen. The Bible is filled with examples of what occurs when people team together. For example, in Matthew 18:19-20 Jesus said, "Again, I tell you that if two of you on earth agree about anything you ask for, it will be done for you by my Father in heaven. For where two or three come together in my name, there am I with them." What an incredible promise—it assures us that there is power in corporate prayer. And as the number of people who pray increases, so does the power of their prayer. As it says in Deuteronomy 32:30, "How could one man chase a thousand, or two put ten thousand to flight, unless their Rock had sold them, unless the LORD had given them up?" God is with us when we pray together, and what happens as a result can be awesome.

BENEFITS OF A PRAYER PARTNER MINISTRY

I'm guessing that you probably recognize the benefit of bringing a group of people together to pray. But you may still be wondering whether you should go through the steps of forming an actual prayer partner ministry in your church. Let me put to rest any remaining doubts you may have by telling you a few of the specific benefits you'll receive from having such a ministry in your church.

- **IT MAKES PRAYER A TOP PRIORITY IN THE CHURCH:** Most churches teach about the importance of prayer and encourage people to pray. But let's face it—most churches do not have an effective, organized prayer ministry. Prayer gets pushed onto the back burner because most people don't see it as vital or exciting. But once a church has a prayer partner ministry, the people begin to understand the importance of prayer and the thrill of witnessing God's answers, especially if the pastor gives the ministry high visibility. As the congregation gets enthusiastic and starts talking to God more and more, prayer goes from a back burner afterthought to a red-hot priority.

- **IT CREATES A FARM TEAM FOR SPIRITUAL LEADERS:** You learn a lot about people when you pray with them, especially about their spiritual maturity. I found that to be true when I prayed with my prayer partners every week. And I also found that as people prayed with me, they began to develop a heart for God similar to mine. As a result, I often looked to my prayer partners when I wanted to develop people for leadership within the church. For example, all the people who became members of Skyline's local board of administration during my ministry were prayer partners first. And some of them continue to work alongside of me at my current ministry, INJOY.

- **IT ENHANCES THE LEADER'S PERSONAL MINISTRY:** The only leader in history who didn't need others to pray for Him was Jesus. He prayed for Himself, and when God intercedes no one else is necessary. But everyone else can benefit from a prayer partner ministry. A pastor who has others praying for him has the potential to go farther than he could ever go alone.

- **IT BLESSES THE PRAYER PARTNERS:** People who become a part of a prayer partner ministry grow spiritually and become closer to God. They also develop strong relationships with others. Skyline prayer partner Larry Doyle said, "Through prayer partners, I met people I had never had lunch with, never played golf with, never really done anything with. But in prayer partners, we shared a special love for each other. There is no other way to develop relationships like that so quickly." Partnering in prayer is always a win-win situation.

- **IT CREATES AN ATMOSPHERE WHERE GOD CAN WORK:** Over the last several years, I've had the privilege of speaking to many thousands of people in conferences, seminars, churches, and even stadiums. Time after time I've seen God do great things. But it's not because of me. The atmosphere of openness to God I witnessed was created by the requests and intercession of my faithful prayer partners. As a result, God was able to do a work. That prayer covering continues even today. Although I no longer have the 120 prayer partners at Skyline Church praying for me, there are now over three hundred prayer partners praying daily for me and INJOY. And the blessings continue.

HOW TO GET A PRAYER PARTNER MINISTRY STARTED

Because the prayer partner ministries that have supported me have been large and powerful, you may feel that starting a prayer partner ministry in your church is too big a job. It's not; if you believe in the power of prayer, you can do it. Here are some guidelines to get you started:

1. Get the Pastor on Board

The first critical step in creating a prayer partners ministry is to get your pastor on board. You saw what happened to Doug Bennett when he approached pastors who didn't want a prayer partner ministry (see chapter 7). God later answered Doug's prayer, but he had to move him to another church to do it. It may be possible to start a prayer partner ministry without the pastor's blessing, but I've never yet seen that happen.

If you are a layman, begin by asking God to show your pastor his need for prayer and make him receptive to a prayer partner ministry. Then, when you believe the time is right, approach your pastor about it. If you are a pastor, then search your heart: Are you willing to let the laypeople of your church come alongside you and partner with you in prayer? If you are willing, you and your church have great days ahead of you.

2. Develop a Pastor-Layman Personal Prayer Partnership

For a prayer partner ministry to develop, there is one relationship that first needs to be established—a partnership between the pastor and a committed layperson who will become his personal intercessor and accountability partner. This critical relationship can be initiated by the layperson (as it was with Bill Klassen for me and Doug Bennett for Bill Rudd) or it can be initiated by the pastor. Most effective prayer partner ministries begin with a personal partnership between these two people and then grow slowly from there.

The layperson who partners with the pastor should desire to do three things for him faithfully and cheerfully:

- **SUPPORT THE PASTOR AND CHURCH:** The person must have a vision for the pastor's ministry, be devoted to his leadership, be supportive of him personally, and have a heart for the church.
- **INTERCEDE FOR THE PASTOR:** He must feel a strong desire to intercede for the pastor and pray for him on a daily basis.
- **KEEP THE PASTOR ACCOUNTABLE:** He must be willing to develop a relationship of mutual accountability where the two can tell each other anything in confidence,

with honesty. This kind of relationship takes time to develop, but the seeds of trust must be there in the beginning. And of course, the pastor and the layperson must be of the same gender. You should never allow an intimate prayer relationship to develop between members of the opposite sex—unless, of course, they're married to each other.

Accountability is an important part of the relationship between the pastor and the personal prayer partner. When Bill Klassen and I met while I was still pastor at Skyline, he always asked me these five questions:

- Do you have a fresh word from the Lord (from personal time with God)?
- Are you walking in obedience to every word of God?
- Are you misusing your authority in the church?
- Is your thought life pure?
- Have you lied about any of the above?

As you develop your own relationship, develop your own set of questions which address the areas where the two of you most need accountability and prayer. You'll find that accountability not only strengthens you for ministry, but it builds your relationship and desire to pray for one another.

3. Recruit Additional Prayer Partners

Once a firm relationship has been established between the pastor and his personal prayer and accountability partner, it's time to begin looking for others to join the prayer team. It's all right to start slow. If you have a very small church, you might find two or three others who desire to pray. Or you may be able to find seven, so that they can each have a day of the week to intercede. No matter where you start, as the prayer partner ministry grows and becomes more visible in the church, additional people will be encouraged to participate.

I used to do a number of things to make prayer partners highly visible at Skyline. For example, I talked about them frequently from the pulpit, thanking and praising them for their dedication. And every Sunday one of them prayed for the offering, so they were always in front of the congregation.

I found that the best way to establish a core of people to pray is to schedule a prayer partner retreat once a year and invite people with potential to attend. (See appendix A for information on how to plan a prayer partner retreat.) When deciding who to invite to the retreat, my personal prayer partner and I targeted four different types of people:

- **THE HOT LIST:** We always invited people in the church who were hot for God. Many of them were older and had walked with God for many years. I particularly enjoyed including the gray-haired saints; some of them might have lacked physical strength, but they possessed great strength spiritually.
- **THE HIT LIST:** Learning to pray more effectively can transform a Christian's life. Often when we identified Christians who lacked maturity but in whom we saw a desire to grow, we'd ask them to be part of the prayer team. Being around some of the more experienced spiritual leaders helped the less mature ones learn and grow.
- **THE HOPE LIST:** My hope list consisted of people with tremendous leadership potential who I wanted to give some time to grow. Paul warned Timothy not to put anyone into a leadership position too soon (1 Tim. 3:6). That's good advice. I got to know my people well by spending a year praying with them before asking them to be leaders. By praying with them regularly, I could sense whether their

hearts were right with God and if they were ready for a leadership position.

- **THE WHOEVER LIST:** Finally, besides selecting particular people to invite to the retreat, we also opened up the ministry to anyone in the congregation who wished to participate. And many times God provided faithful prayer warriors that we would have otherwise overlooked. However, if you will be starting with a very small group of prayer partners, you may want to wait until the ministry is firmly established and growing before opening it up to everyone in the congregation. In his book *Prayer Shield,* my friend C. Peter Wagner points out that prayer and intercession "seems to be a magnet for emotionally disturbed people." So discernment should be used, especially when getting started.

After we determined who we would invite, we held the annual retreat, where everyone spent the day praying and learning about prayer. At the end of the day, we passed out commitment cards and allowed each person to decide whether God was calling him to become a prayer partner for the coming year. (See appendix C for a sample prayer partner commitment form.) Anyone who did agreed to the following five commitments:

1. Become a member of the church, if you are not one already.
2. Attend the quarterly prayer partner breakfasts.
3. Attend the annual prayer partner retreat.
4. Pray daily for the church and its staff. Pray for specific needs on an assigned day of the week or month. (See appendix C for suggestions.)
5. Come to the church on each assigned Sunday to join other prayer partners and pray for the pastor, the church, and the service.

I should note at this point that although my current prayer partners include both men and women, when I was the senior pastor at Skyline Church, I invited only men to be my prayer partners. That wasn't because I didn't recognize women's ability to pray. In fact, in most churches, women pray more than men do. My decision was motivated by a couple of reasons: First, because men have often neglected to step forward as spiritual leaders on their own, I wanted to use the prayer partner ministry to help them develop spiritually. Second, I have always taken special care to avoid situations that are likely to tempt me morally. I don't pray, dine, or travel alone with a person of the opposite sex—except for my wife, Margaret. I don't ever want to put myself or my prayer partners in an awkward position or a place where they might become tempted.

As you form a prayer partner ministry, you may not feel it's necessary to restrict the prayer team to all women or all men. But if you do decide to have members of the opposite sex praying together, be very sensitive to these issues.

4. Get the Prayer Partners Organized

Once you have a group of people willing to pray, it's important to organize them so that they can pray most effectively. At Skyline, the person who fulfilled this role was the prayer partner coordinator He provided administrative leadership to the team and functioned as the primary communication link between the pastor and the prayer partners. For many years Bill Klassen, my personal prayer partner, filled that role. Later, board member and friend, Bill Laugaland (and then Dennis Suchecki) oversaw the ministry.

The logical person to fill this role is usually the pastor's personal prayer partner, but someone else could be chosen to do it. What's important is that the person be a recognized spiritual leader with a consistent prayer life, a heart for the pastor and church, and organizational ability. His primary duties include creating monthly prayer schedules and guides that let the prayer partners know when and how to pray, communicating special prayer needs and praises, and assisting the pastor and his staff with the quarterly breakfasts and annual retreat. (See appendix C for sample schedules and letters.)

5. Plan for Prayer Partners to Pray for Every Service

The heart of any prayer partner ministry is the time of prayer before and during each of the church's services. Each Sunday a group should come to the church about forty-five minutes to an hour before the starting time of the service (according to the prayer partner coordinator's schedule). Once there, they should do the following:

- **PRAY GEOGRAPHICALLY:** For about the first twenty minutes, they should lay hands on everything in the sanctuary—the pulpit, the piano, and the pews—asking God to make everything work according to His plan and to bless and minister to the people who will soon be there.

- **PRAY FOR THE PASTOR:** About twenty-five minutes or so before the service begins, they should move to a private area with the pastor, possibly his office, to pray for him. Before they begin, the pastor should share any requests he has and tell them about any answers to prayer that he's received.

- **PRAY DURING THE CHURCH SERVICE:** As the service begins, the prayer partners should retreat to an area near the sanctuary and pray for the service. When my prayer partners first began at Skyline, they had difficulty praying for a full hour. So we began leaving them a prayer agenda. (See the sample Sunday Morning Prayer Guide in appendix C.) As time went by they gained confidence, and their prayer time became more spontaneous.

6. Keep the Momentum Going

Maintaining a vital prayer partner ministry requires several things: Periodic instruction in prayer, the ongoing development of relationships among prayer partners, and continued motivation for them to pray. At Skyline we accomplished these goals through our annual retreat and quarterly prayer partner breakfasts. (See appendix B for how to plan a quarterly breakfast.) I taught a new lesson every time we met, and we set aside time for everyone to meet and pray with other prayer partners. We shared answers to prayer and praised everyone for their valuable contributions. Skyline prayer partner Ben Grame said, "I always felt uplifted at the meetings because John gave people credit. His appreciation made me want to move forward in prayer."

Nothing motivates like victory, and when you start a prayer partner ministry in your church, you will experience many victories. I recently asked Doug Bennett to share with me some of the things that have happened since he began a prayer partner ministry with his pastor, Bill Rudd, back in Michigan. He told me about many of the wonderful benefits to the church and the pastor. Doug said, "There is a unity in the church unlike anything we've ever seen before. People are working together as a team. The older and younger generations are coming together and getting to know one another better. And the pastor's life has changed; he no longer feels that he's bearing the burden alone. He's experiencing greater victory over temptation, and he's preaching with greater power and freedom."

"What about the people who are praying?" I asked.

"Oh, their experiences have been wonderful," Doug answered. "The impact that this ministry has had on individual lives—it's something I never expected. When I first talked about starting a prayer partner ministry, I was told, 'You'll get lots of people who are willing to pray, but don't expect any men!' But the men did step forward to pray, and I've seen tremendous changes in marriages and families. They've developed relationships on a much deeper level than just talking about ball scores. As a matter of fact, within months they've built relationships that normally take decades to develop. It's incredible!'"

He then shared with me a testimonial he recently received from a prayer partner. Here's what it said:

> I've been involved in prayer partners for about a year now, and my life has really changed: my marriage has grown, my financial situation has improved, and my spiritual life has matured. My time praying has brought me back to the realization that God is real, that Jesus is real, and that my former life was not what I really wanted.
>
> I am much happier than I used to be. My prayer life is by far much better than it has ever been. It is so exciting to pray for others in need and watch God work miracles that I never thought possible. The Bible tells us all we need to do is ask and we will receive. The world is full of people who don't even know who to ask, let alone how! It is an honor to be involved in a ministry that we can literally watch change lives.
>
> When I got involved as a prayer partner, I had no idea how powerful prayer could be. The results of my personal prayer have been incredible. I could not have imagined the results in my wildest dreams. I pray daily that this ministry will reach into every corner of this country so that it can be a God-fearing land once again.

I believe God is beginning to answer that prayer. And you may even be a part of it. If your church and pastor already have a prayer partner ministry, get involved. If not, maybe you should be the one to start a prayer partner ministry in your church. Think about it, and start praying. It may be God's desire to answer the prayer of this brother in Christ by sending *you!*

DISCUSSION QUESTIONS

1. How would an organized prayer partner ministry change your church? What might you see happen?

2. If your pastor were considering inviting you to a prayer partner retreat, would you be on one of his recruiting lists? If so, which one? Why?
   a. The Hot List (hot for God)
   b. The Hit List (needing to grow as a Christian)
   c. The Hope List (a potential leader wanting to grow)
   d. The Whoever List (a heart to pray for the pastor)

3. How high a priority would you judge prayer to be in your church currently?
   a. at a red-hot boil
   b. strongly simmering
   c. lukewarm on the back burner
   d. ice-cold—not even on the stove

4. How could you help to turn up the heat on prayer in your church?

5. What would it take to get a prayer partner ministry started in your church? Who might be called to step forward and start the process?

AFTERWORD: ANTICIPATING REVIVAL

If my people, who are called by my name, will humble themselves
and pray and seek my face and turn from their wicked ways,
then will I hear from heaven and will forgive their sin
and will heal their land.

2 Chronicles 7:14

What *will* it take for God to reach every corner of this country and make it a God-fearing land again? I believe the answer is revival. I mentioned in chapter 7 that I rededicated my life to Christ and answered the call to preach during a seven-week revival at my home church in Circleville, Ohio. It happened when I was seventeen years old. I'll never forget what it was like: Over three hundred people got saved during those weeks.

Today there's a lot of talk among Christians about revival and how much it's needed; it's almost become a buzzword in some Christian circles. But what is it really, and do we really need it? I once read a definition that said: "Revival is something that nobody can explain but everyone recognizes when it gets there."

Dr. Armin Gesswein saw revival this way:

> The revival we need is simply a return to normal New Testament Christianity, where the churches are full of prayer, full of power, full of people, full of praise, full of divine happenings all the time. We want something normal, not just 'special.' God's normal, that is. God's normal is greater than most of our specials put together.

Revival isn't a process that people can use to manipulate God. You cannot *plan* a true revival, but you can *seek* it. I've found that God-ordained revival follows a pattern. Here's what I've observed:

1. The people pray.
2. God comes.
3. The people repent.
4. God revives the people.
5. The people begin to minister to and pour their lives into others.
6. God equips and empowers them, making up the difference.

Revival can come—but it all begins with prayer.

Any time God is going to do something wonderful, He begins with a difficulty. When He is going to do something *very* wonderful, He begins with an *impossibility*. If you look around today, I think you'll agree that our country seems to be in an impossible situation. Only God will be able to save our churches, our families, and our nation. And He will come if we begin to pray. It's time for us to get started.

APPENDICES:

How to Start a Prayer Partner Ministry in Your Home Church

PLANNING YOUR PRAYER PARTNER RETREAT

Come with me by yourselves to a quiet place
and get some rest.
Mark 6:31

The annual retreat is an important part of any prayer partner ministry. Speaking about the retreat, longtime prayer partner Dick Hausam said:

> I always looked forward to them. They were so awesome and uplifting. I'll never forget the times when we opened up to each other. John, you always set the tone by confessing first, and the guys would naturally follow. Men would stand up and confess to sexual sin, alcohol abuse, et cetera, and bawl like babies. Others would stand up and say, "Last year I stood up and received prayer for this. I received victory, and now I'm going to pray for you." We were cleaning out the dirt before we went to the altar. It was at the first retreat that I saw you in a different light, John; as a real person, instead of just the shepherd of the flock.

The prayer partner retreat is the catalyst for your prayer partner ministry. It's an excellent time to learn *how* to pray, practice what you've learned, connect with other prayer partners, and strengthen your relationship with God.

The retreat serves one other very important purpose: vision-casting. For new recruits, this will be their first exposure to partnering with the pastor through prayer. To cast the vision effectively, you must show them the value of praying for their pastor, so that they are passionate about it and willing to commit. For veteran prayer partners, vision-casting will serve to renew their passion, reminding them of the joy they've already received, and exciting them about the ministry for the coming year.

WHERE TO HOLD YOUR RETREAT

A group retreat, just like a solo retreat, should be held *away from* familiar surroundings to avoid distractions and provide privacy.

Don't meet on or near the church property if you can possibly avoid it. In choosing your site, take the following into account:

- **DISTANCE:** Find a location that's far enough from the church to feel special, but not so far that it's inconvenient. Any location that requires more than an hour's drive is probably too far.
- **PRIVACY AND QUIET:** The fewer the distractions, the better. Privacy makes it easier for everyone to be vulnerable before God and each other. And in peace and quiet, you will be able to listen and pray more effectively.
- **COMFORT:** Participants will be in one place for quite a few hours, so find a site with comfortable seating, good lighting, rest rooms nearby, and efficient temperature control. Make sure heating and/or air-conditioning (depending on the time of year) actually *work*. Retreat centers and hotel meeting rooms are specifically designed to meet this criteria, and the town hall or local college might also be able to provide a good room. But if none of those fits your needs or budget, feel free to be creative

For years, Skyline's prayer partner retreat took place in the fellowship hall of another local church in our denomination. In exchange, we offered them the use of our facilities for some of their functions. This served as both a low-priced option *and* a goodwill gesture between congregations. You might be able to make a similar arrangement with a church in your area.

WHEN TO HAVE YOUR RETREAT

A prayer partner retreat should be scheduled either once or twice a year. At Skyline, we held it annually on a Saturday, and it lasted all day (8 A.M. to 3 P.M.). The best time of year to hold it depends on your church's annual schedule. Most churches are more active from early autumn (after school starts) through New Year's Day. Things tend to be the slowest, and attendance the lowest, in the middle of summer. Avoid either extreme. When your members are gone on vacation, you won't get the response you could during high attendance periods. And during hectic times, many people will be unable to fit another commitment on their calendars.

At Skyline, we found that the school schedule provided natural transition times for the entire family, when people were eager to join something new. Our best time to "kick off" a new area of involvement was just before school started and after everyone returned from their summer vacations (late August-early September). Another good time for us was early summer—after school got out, but before people left on vacation.

Here are some other variables to take into account:

- **WEATHER:** Use common sense in this area. If your summers are sweltering, and your location doesn't have air-conditioning, don't have your retreat in July. If your entire congregation is regularly snowed in during winter, don't choose February.
- **CONFLICTING CHURCH OR COMMUNITY ACTIVITIES:** Avoid scheduling your retreat in competition with other equally interesting or important events. If you force your people to choose, everyone loses.

FOOD AND FELLOWSHIP AT A RETREAT

Before participants can relate to God together, they must be able to relate to each other. They need a casual, friendly environment, where interaction is easy and natural. One of the best ways to provide this atmosphere is through food and fellowship times.

Skyline prayer partner retreats typically began with an opportunity for the participants to talk while enjoying coffee, juice, and doughnuts for thirty minutes before the program began. They were also provided with lunch at the retreat and were encouraged to spend time getting to know one another while they ate.

COMPONENTS FOR A POWERFUL RETREAT

1. Vision-Casting by the Leader

Many participants at the retreat won't be sure exactly what prayer partners are or why they are at the retreat. By casting vision first, you answer their questions and prepare them for the rest of the day's agenda. As mentioned before, vision-casting stirs a passion for prayer partner ministry, unifying participants and making them eager to commit to praying for their pastor.

2. Prayer Training and Modeling for the Partners

Every retreat should include some training and modeling, no matter how experienced the participants are. Teach on a prayer-related topic, such as intercession, fasting, praise, laying on of hands, how to have a quiet time, praying Scripture, etc. The best way to learn about prayer is by *doing*, so be sure to reinforce what is taught during corporate prayer.

3. The Pastor Expresses Prayer Requests for Himself and the Church

Preparation for prayer begins here, as the pastor shares prayer needs for himself, his family, and the church. The more specific and transparent the pastor can be, the better. One of the first steps of corporate revival occurs when the leader stands before the people and admits that he is not able to do the work on his own and needs their and God's help.

The pastor should then give the people some uninterrupted time to ask God which requests He is calling them to pray for during the coming year.

4. The Partners Make Their Prayer Requests

This time of confession is the most important part of the retreat, and if the pastor has been transparent before the prayer partners, they will readily follow his example. Allowing them to confess their needs helps the pastor know how to pray for them. Plus, others at the retreat are encouraged as they realize that they are not alone in their imperfections. Through corporate confession, God breaks in and renews the hearts of His people.

5. The Pastor Prays for the Partners

Participants need to hear their leader pray for them, since it demonstrates that he cares for them. Plus, it is an incredibly cleansing and encouraging time. Both pastor and partners experience great joy as the pastor asks God to meet their spiritual needs.

Whenever someone confesses, ask if anyone else is struggling with the same issue. Have everyone with the same struggle stand up, and pray for them right then.

6. The Partners Pray for Each Other

After the pastor prays for the partners, have each of them choose one other prayer partner and commit to pray for him for the rest of the year. Encourage them to be accountable to each other, and give them time to get together, share, and pray in groups of three or four.

7. Everyone Prays for the Church

Finish the prayer time by focusing on the needs of the church. This refocuses the vision on the big picture for the coming year. Pray for specific needs, from budget issues to upcoming events to staff needs. Ask for specific answers from God. As the prayer partners see God's answers to these prayers, their passion will be fueled throughout the year.

8. The Partners Commit to Pray for the Next Year

After participants have heard the vision and experienced the Spirit's work through prayer together, ask them to make a decision about joining (or continuing) this ministry for the coming year. Clearly explain all qualifications and responsibilities. (See appendix C for the Prayer Partner Commitment form that was used at Skyline.)

9. Planning for the Year

Give the prayer partners a schedule for the year, including upcoming prayer breakfasts, special events, and prayer emphases (see appendix C for samples). Also assign one day on which they will pray all day for the pastor and the church. The frequency needed will depend on the size of your group. For example, if your group is small, you might assign a day of the week. If it is large, a day of the month will work. At Skyline, each prayer partner was asked to pray throughout the day one day each month on the date that corresponded to his birthday (e.g., someone born on March 10 would pray on the tenth of each month).

NOTE TO THE PASTOR: DOING WHAT ONLY YOU CAN DO

As the leader, you set the tone for all interaction that takes place at the retreat. The prayer partnership can benefit you and your ministry, but it will only be as effective as you allow it to be. If you don't share your struggles as well as your successes, your partners will not know how to pray for you. If you are unfriendly or aloof, your partners, following your model, will not bond during fellowship, and group prayer will fall flat. If you aren't willing to thank them and acknowledge the value of their prayers, they will lose motivation and passion.

Your prayer partners will always follow your example, so you are responsible for making the first move in every area. Your modeling is especially important in the following areas:

1. UNITY: Spend time getting to know each person, letting them know you love them. Introduce people with common interests, and help them get to know each other.

2. APPRECIATION: Never stop thanking your prayer partners for their ministry to you. Celebrate the victories that come as a direct result of their prayers. Always communicate that their individual and corporate prayers are essential to the success of your church

3. TRANSPARENCY: If you are going to develop lasting relationships with your prayer partners, transparency is fundamental. When you are transparent, you communicate that you trust and value them and their prayers. By confessing your sins, needs, and weaknesses, you show them how they can pray for you. And you open the door for them to be transparent too.

APPENDIX

B

PREPARING PRAYER PARTNER BREAKFASTS

L ike any ministry, a prayer partnership needs the ongoing encouragement provided by regular times together. Dennis Suchecki, who was my prayer partner coordinator for many years at Skyline, said of our quarterly prayer breakfasts, "It was so good to be with everyone at the breakfasts. We always got a lot out of Pastor John's lessons on prayer, and I often found ways to quickly apply the principles he taught. Another thing that really touched my heart was our worship time. While we sang worship and praise choruses, I took the time to just listen to the other men. What a blessing to hear so many men's voices blended in praise to God! How God must have loved it."

The prayer partner breakfasts are nourishment for a prayer partner ministry. Prayer partners literally empty themselves every day, lifting their pastors and church before the Lord, and they need to be "filled back up" on a periodic basis. Regular prayer breakfasts help both participants and pastors to share in fellowship, support, and prayer, which strengthens their bond to each other and motivates them to continue in the ministry.

WHERE TO HOLD YOUR BREAKFAST

Unlike the retreat, a prayer partner breakfast *can* be held on the church property. I recommend a private, quiet room, just large enough for the number expected. The tables should be set up so that participants can: 1) enjoy comfortable fellowship as they eat; 2) participate in worship; and 3) see and hear whoever is speaking or leading worship.

Locate your meeting close enough to where the food is prepared, but not so close that the sounds in the kitchen cause distraction. You might even consider eating together in one room and then moving to another, more private, room for the rest of the meeting.

WHEN TO HAVE YOUR BREAKFAST

Prayer partner breakfasts should occur on a Saturday morning, no less often than once a quarter. As you select the date, take your church's annual schedule into account, and try to plan breakfasts during slower times of the year. Don't schedule a breakfast in competition with some other church or community activity, since it will force participants to choose one over the other.

At Skyline, we met early in the morning (8:00-10:30 A.M.), in order to dismiss early and let participants have the rest of the day free

COMPONENTS OF AN ENCOURAGING BREAKFAST

1. Food and Fellowship (60 Minutes)

Times of food and fellowship are excellent for establishing easy and natural interaction, which is essential to helping the prayer partners develop relationships with one another. Thus, the *breakfast* component of the meeting is very important. Make sure to provide enough time for a casual, leisurely breakfast, and encourage participants to get to know one another better.

2. Worship (15 Minutes)

Worship is the best way to prepare people's hearts to hear God's Word and to pray, since it naturally draws them closer to Him. Before worship begins, challenge the prayer partners to open their hearts to God and listen for His voice during your time together.

3. Equipping (45 Minutes)

After every quarterly breakfast, the prayer partners should come away with a better understanding of at least one aspect of prayer. The pastor or another leader should share an in-depth lesson focused on helping participants grow in their prayer life. Some good topics include praise, thanksgiving, intercession, meditation, listening to God, praying Scripture, etc.

Make sure the lesson gives prayer partners some specific truths to think about and apply in the coming months.

4. Prayer (30 Minutes)

Since the focus of this ministry is on prayer, it should always be the last thing you do together. This encourages and inspires the prayer partners to continue supporting their church in this way. While still in one large group, share some recent answers to prayer, since this reminds participants of the results and value of their ministry. Then list current prayer requests for the pastors and the church.

Divide everyone into small prayer groups of three or four. First, remind them of how they can apply the day's lesson to this prayer time. Ask them to share personal prayer requests for five to ten minutes. Then they will pray for the church, the pastors, and each other for twenty to thirty minutes. Since every small group tends to finish at a different time, I recommend telling them they are dismissed when their group has finished praying. Before breaking up into these small prayer clusters, close the large group with prayer yourself.

C

CREATING PRAYER PARTNER GUIDES AND LETTERS

For a prayer partner ministry to succeed, open and frequent communication is important. Prayer partners need current, structured information in order to pray effectively. They also need direction and guidance on *how* to pray for their pastor.

Besides the training they receive at retreats and breakfasts, your prayer partners should receive a monthly packet from the prayer partner coordinator. It should include a personal letter, thanking them for their ministry, along with instruction on how to pray for the pastor and church for the current month. At Skyline, our prayer partner coordinator also often enclosed interesting or informative articles on prayer that he had collected.

The following pages contain explanations and samples of the materials necessary to inform and guide your church's prayer partners in their ministry.

1. THE PRAYER PARTNER COMMITMENT RESPONSE (distributed at the annual retreat)

2. GUIDES FOR DIFFERENT TYPES OF PRAYER
Daily Prayer
Periodic Intensive Prayer
Prayer During the Sunday Service
Voluntary Prayer for the Offering

3. SAMPLE LETTERS
Invitation to the annual retreat
Invitation to a quarterly prayer breakfast
Monthly letter of encouragement and information

THE PRAYER PARTNER COMMITMENT

Without a doubt, our church is on the verge of greater things than we have ever seen. As we move forward, we must have a strong, faithful prayer base. Thank you for your interest in being a prayer partner.

We invite you to commit to a ministry that will capture your heart, increase your vision, and draw you toward deeper spiritual devotion. God's desire for each prayer partner is to develop a vital, fresh prayer ministry that permeates your life and your relationships with others.

All great spiritual awakenings and movings of God are preceded by a commitment by individuals and groups to the discipline of prayer. We can anticipate a rewarding year together, as we are accountable to each other in this ministry.

Below are our church's prayer partner commitments. To participate in this exciting ministry, we ask that you commit to the following responsibilities:

1. Become a member of the church, if you are not one already.
2. Attend the quarterly prayer partner breakfasts.
3. Attend the annual prayer partner retreat.
4. Pray daily for the church and its staff. Pray for specific needs on your assigned day of the week/month.
5. On your assigned Sunday to pray, join other prayer partners and the pastor in the prayer room *before* the service. (If you are not available on your assigned Sunday, you are responsible to send another prayer partner as a replacement.) You will exchange prayer requests and pray with the pastor, and then your group will remain to pray throughout the service.

PRAYER PARTNER RESPONSE

Name_____ Phone (H)_____
Address_____   (W)_____
City/State/Zip_____ Birthdate_____

Are you willing to abide by the five prayer partner commitments?

☐ Yes   ☐ No

In which service(s) would you prefer to pray?

☐ 1st   ☐ 2nd   ☐ 3rd   ☐ 4th

Signature:_____
Comments:_____
_____

Personal Prayer Request(s):_____
_____
_____

Personal Praise Report(s):_____
_____
_____

GUIDES FOR DIFFERENT TYPES OF PRAYER

Daily Prayer

MONTHLY GUIDE TO PRAYER FOR YOUR PASTOR

One of the prayer partner commitments is to pray *daily* for the pastor and church. To make it easy for your prayer partners to do this, I recommend that you regularly send them a daily prayer guideline for each month (enclosed with the monthly letter).

You can direct your prayer partners' daily prayer in a variety of ways:

1. As they feel led: This is the most open-ended method. It should only be used for experienced interceders who know the pastor's personal needs well and who don't require much structure. Instruct the prayer partners to ask God for guidance in interceding for the pastor and church. When truly led by the Holy Spirit, they can effectively cover all the needs in prayer.

2. "Top Seven" needs: This provides a little more direction for your prayer partners and also helps them get to know the pastor and his needs. Ask the pastor for a "top seven" list of general prayer requests, for things like "family time," "wisdom," "anointing," etc. Then assign each to a day of the week. On any given day, every prayer partner will lift up the designated need for that day. If your prayer partners have been taught how to pray Scripture, include a biblical reference for them to apply to the pastor's life. Change the Scripture references each month, and the actual requests as needed.

Sample:

Each day of the week, pray for the following areas first for yourself, and then for the pastor. Using the Bible references, pray Scripture by applying God's Word to your and the pastor's life.

Sunday:	Rest and strength	Psalm 23
Monday:	Intimacy with God	2 Corinthians 13:14
Tuesday:	Family	Ephesians 4:32
Wednesday:	Ministry effectiveness	Ephesians 4:11-13
Thursday:	Obedience to God	Luke 9:23-24
Friday:	Leadership	Romans 12:6-8
Saturday:	Wisdom	James 1:5

3. Requests for special events: This method takes prayer partners' involvement one crucial step further. By giving them very specific needs for which to intercede, you're providing the opportunity to see concrete answers to their prayers. This helps prayer partners to grow as intercessors and to bond even more with the pastors.

The prayer partner coordinator should ask the pastors for their schedule for the month. The coordinator can then list the important events and their dates for the prayer partners and ask them to pray specifically for those events on those dates. Your list may be large or small, or vary from month to month. Work with the pastors to decide which items should be listed.

Sample:

Please pray for the specific needs of the pastors and church on the appropriate dates this month.

May 1	That our people attending the ministry information meeting would commit to involvement in a ministry at our church

May 5 (Sun)	Anointing and sensitivity to the Holy Spirit as our senior pastor preaches on stewardship in the morning services
May 12 (Sun)	Stamina and anointed communication as our associate pastor preaches on commitment in the morning services
May 16-18	Safe travel and God's anointing for our senior pastor as he speaks at the denominational conference on evangelism
May 19 (Sun)	Clear vision and wisdom as our senior pastor preaches on evangelism in the morning services
May 25	That our Sunday school teachers would receive and apply practical tools at their training seminar; that our associate pastor would communicate clearly and effectively
May 26 (Sun)	Anointing and openness as our senior pastor preaches on discipleship in the morning services

4. Day-by-day prayer guidance: This is the most thorough method of guidance for your prayer partners. They know exactly what to pray for on a given day; plus they get to know the pastor's heart and vision for the church. The prayer partner coordinator should ask the pastors for a copy of their calendar for the month, then write out a request for each ministry date. A list of ongoing requests then can be inserted in the open dates (see sample below).

It's important for the prayer partner coordinator to be creative and work with the pastor to include needs that reveal his real strengths and weaknesses. For example, if the pastor has Mondays off, but admits that he tends to miss out on family time by filling his Mondays with church concerns, he should insert a "family time" request on each Monday in the prayer calendar.

Sample (one week)
from the prayer guide for John Maxwell's prayer partners:

Please pray the following for John on the appropriate date.

Oct. 30	Clear vision from God for INJOY at their board meeting
Oct. 31	For John to remain dependent on God
Nov. 1	Protection as John travels to Canada
Nov. 2	Anointing as John speaks to a group of executives (Canada); energy and safe travel to Ohio
Nov. 3	That pastors and their churches' lives and ministries would be transformed as a result of attending the INJOY Stewardship Seminar (Ohio); physical stamina and safe travel to Colorado
Nov. 4	Anointing for John; that people attending the INJOY Lay Ministry Seminar (Colorado) commit to involvement in lay ministry in their home churches; protection and stamina for John as he travels to Oklahoma
Nov. 5 (Sun)	A special time of family worship for the Maxwells

Please feel free to adapt these suggestions to your church's and pastor's needs. They work in a variety of combinations. I currently have over three hundred prayer partners across the country who pray for me and INJOY. Four times a year, they receive a prayer guide that combines the day-by-day guide (number 3) with a "top seven" list (number 2). This means that on any given day, my prayer partners are praying for one general request, like "wisdom," along with a specific request for that date.

I recommend that you use the method that helps prayer partners see the heart of the pastor at the deepest level with which he feels comfortable.

In other words, if a pastor is reluctant to reveal many needs at first, respect this preference and instruct prayer partners to pray "as they feel led." Then, as the pastor becomes more comfortable sharing with people, make the requests more specific.

When needs are spelled out in detail, the partnership between pastors and laypeople strengthens. And the answers to specific prayers provide encouragement for everyone involved.

Periodic Intensive Prayer

Besides daily intercession during their time alone with God, ask your prayer partners to commit to one day of intensive prayer per week or month. On their assigned day, your prayer partners should "pray without ceasing" throughout the day, for the pastors and church.

Depending on the size of your group, assign each prayer partner a specific day of the *week* or *month*. Your goal is to have at least one person praying intensively every single day. Thus, the larger the group, the less frequently they need to be assigned.

PRAYER ASSIGNMENTS FOR ONCE A WEEK

For the small- to average-sized group, I recommend that you assign one day of the week to each prayer partner. Even the smallest group can pray effectively in this way, since you only need seven participants to cover the church in prayer. This method works well for any size group, as long as they are committed to pray on a weekly basis.

Sample Weekly Prayer Assignment Sheet
(for a group of 21):

Sundays	Dave Williams
	John Smith
	Tamara Owens
Mondays	Russell Johnson
	Ken Whiteside
	Harry Lee
Tuesdays	Scott Thompson
	Dorothy Avila
	Aaron Mitchell
Wednesdays	Tim Burns
	Vince Collier
	Stuart Kendall
Thursdays	Ken Miller
	Kevin McDougal
	Darrell Washington
Fridays	Victor Martinez
	Wendy Van Huyk
	Marty Stanislaski
Saturdays	Rodney Culver
	John Dennison
	Bill Jones

PRAYER ASSIGNMENTS FOR ONCE A MONTH

Once your group numbers at least thirty-one, you can transition into a monthly prayer commitment. Ask prayer partners to pray throughout the day on a specific *date* of every month (e.g., the fifteenth).

Sample Monthly Prayer Assignment Sheet

1	Stuart Ingram	17	Mario Bautista
2	Todd Williams	18	Rodney Gray
3	Alice Culbertson	19	Denise Munoz
4	Herb Barnett	20	Oscar Porter
5	Tom Goode	21	Leonard Wallace
6	Ron Hanson	22	Bruce Marshall
7	Larry Woo	23	Joanne Christianson
8	Art Sorensen	24	Max Singer
9	Dale Hoover	25	Victor Sanchez
10	Sandra Garcia	26	Gene Eldridge
11	Dave Hopper	27	Andrew Bennett
12	Simone Lange	28	Gordon Moore
13	Marv Van Sykes	29	Marty Washington
14	Ben Graham	30	Cheryl Jones
15	Lee Rothmoor	31	Darrell Best
16	Kevin O'Brien		

MONTHLY PRAYER ASSIGNMENT SHEET—BY BIRTHDAY

Prayer partner teams that number over 100 have another fun option. At Skyline, we asked our prayer partners to pray on the date of their birthday. For example, if a person was born on December 5, he or she would pray on the fifth of every month. Since most people tend to remember their own birthdays, this worked really well. With a group of 100 or more, all the days of the month are usually covered

Prayer During the Sunday Service

When prayer partners gather to pray on Sunday mornings, they offer support to their pastors in the same way that Aaron and Hur supported Moses in the battle with the Amalekites. As the pastor delivers God's Word to the people, he is able to rest in the knowledge that in some room at or near the church, two or more are gathered together to lift up the ministry in prayer.

The prayer partner coordinator should assign at least two prayer partners for every Sunday morning service and designate one as the captain. How often each person will pray will depend on the size of your group.

Sample One-Month Prayer Schedule
Large Church (50 or more partners)

In this example, with three morning services, five prayer partners can be assigned to every service. Most members serve just once a month; only a few names appear twice.

First Service	Second Service	Third Service
	January 7	
*Todd Williams	*Alice Culbertson	*Art Sorensen
+Sandra Garcia	+Ben Graham	+Larry Woo
Deanne Hoff	Rhonda Hartson	Kevin O'Brien
Simone Lange	Dale Hoover	Mario Bautista
Marv Van Sykes	Lee Rothmoor	Rodney Gray
	January 14	
*Victor Sanchez	*Joanne Christianson	*Gordon Moore
+Oscar Porter	+Max Singer	+Marty Washington
Leonard Wallace	Denise Munoz	Gene Eldridge
Bruce Marshall	Cheryl Jones	Darrell Best
Kenny Walton	Andrew Bennett	Jimmy Weston

First Service	Second Service	Third Service
	January 21	
*John Elias	*Skip Dubranski	*Gary Jenkins
+Bob Smith	+Dale Hoover	+Sergio Duran
Paul Sousa	Russell Morgan	Art Sorensen
Mark Miller	Bob Navarro	Larry Woo
Victor Sanchez	Alec Jackson	Stan Wilson
	January 28	
*Dwayne Owens	*Dave Hopper	*Tom Goode
+Bruce Marshall	+Stuart Ingram	+Dan Kelly
Scott Collins	Judy Levine	Jimmy Weston
Leonard Wallace	Beatrice Delgado	Charles Lee
Herb Barnett	Alice Culbertson	Cordell Shaw

    * Prayer captain
    + Person praying for offering during the service

Sample One-Month Prayer Schedule
Medium-sized Church (12 partners)

Members of this size ministry team serve twice a month in groups of three. As in any size group, they can rotate as "Captain" as needed.

First Service	Second Service
January 7	
*Dave Williams	*John Smith
+Tamara Owens	+Russell Johnson
Ken Whiteside	Harry Lee
January 14	
*Scott Thompson	*Dorothy Avila
+Aaron Mitchell	+Tim Burns
Vince Collier	Stuart Kendall

First Service	**Second Service**

January 21

First Service	Second Service
*Ken Whiteside	*Tamara Owens
+Dave Williams	+John Smith
Harry Lee	Russell Johnson

January 28

First Service	Second Service
*Vince Collier	*Tim Burns
+Scott Thompson	+Dorothy Avila
Aaron Mitchell	Stuart Kendall

* Prayer captain
\+ Person praying for offering during the service

Sample One-Month Prayer Schedule
Small Church (8 partners)

January 7	January 21
*Dave Jacobs	*Ken Miller
+Tim Ainsler	+Stan Lukowski
January 14	**January 28**
*Scott Patterson	*Vince Collier
+Aaron Mitchell	+Russell Jackson

* Prayer captain
\+ Person praying for offering during the service

Prayer During the Sunday Service

Sample Sunday Morning Prayer Guide

November 26, 1989

THIS MORNING:

Pastor Joe's sermon is entitled, "Peace for the Holiday Pace." Pray that we would all keep our perspective during this hectic season.

THIS EVENING:

The choir will present "A Festival of Christmas," a beautiful candlelight service featuring traditional Christmas music.

PRAYER REQUESTS:

- That we continue to meet our budgeted needs
- Living Christmas tree preparation (wisdom and physical strength for the director and staff, safety during construction, health for the cast and crew, and audience members who are not Christians)
- Continued attitude of personal and corporate revival
- Continued dependence on God through prayer
- Holidays are sometimes difficult for the elderly, lonely, and widowed. Pray for God's comfort and encouragement to be revealed in the lives of those who need His touch.

MISSIONARIES OF THE MONTH:

Don and Paula Denison, and Butch and Susie Waltholtz
Reminder:
Our next breakfast is scheduled for Saturday, January 27, 8:00 A.M., in the Centre.

Voluntary Prayer for the Offering

Sample Guide to Offertory Prayer

On the monthly prayer schedule, one prayer partner is normally assigned to pray for the offering for each service. If you are given this assignment, please heed the following guidelines.

PROCEDURE:

1. Before the service, meet your prayer captain to let him know you are still available to pray. If you are substituting for someone else, communicate this to him.
2. The offertory prayer occurs during the first fifteen to twenty minutes of the service, so you should enter the auditorium as the service begins. Sit on an aisle in the audience near the platform.
3. During the fellowship time, when people are standing and greeting each other, leave your seat and make your way onto the platform.
4. Introduce yourself to the worship leader as the person praying for the offering. If you are substituting for another prayer partner, be sure to communicate that, in order to be properly introduced.
5. As the worship leader steps to the microphone, stand back from him/her, but no more than ten feet away, so you can quickly advance to the pulpit when called upon.
6. After you pray, leave the platform and the auditorium, and join the other prayer partners for the rest of the service in the prayer room.

PRAYER GUIDELINES:

- **Be Prepared:** Preparation will give you confidence and diminish "stage fright." But be aware that your prayer will sound unnatural if you overprepare. Don't write out or overly rehearse your prayer. Instead, plan *roughly* what you will say, and allow the Holy Spirit to lead you.
- **Be Yourself:** Don't try to be more eloquent than you really are. Remember that you don't need to impress God with your command of the language, and He's the one you're talking to. Also, your prayer should encourage, not bore, the congregation.

Use simple words and short phrases. And stop talking when you run out of things to say.

- **Be Brief:** Remember that your purpose is to share a brief offertory prayer, not to deliver a sermonette, share a Scripture, or give a testimony.

Although praying before a large group can be intimidating, it is also very rewarding. The more often you do it, the more natural it becomes. And not only will you enjoy representing the congregation before the Lord, but you'll also experience incredible personal growth.

SAMPLE LETTERS
Invitation to Prayer Partner Breakfast

Dear Prayer Partner,

Our next prayer partner breakfast is scheduled for Saturday, January 27, at 8:00 A.M. in the Centre. We'll have a great time of food and fellowship, followed by wonderful worship. Then Pastor Bob will share a great lesson on prayer principles. And of course, we will have a chance to pray together as an entire group.

I hope you can join us. It will be a wonderful time of ministry and growth. Please call the church secretary with your reservation.

Sincerely,

Ken Miller
Prayer Partner Coordinator

Invitation to Prayer Partner Retreat

Dear Prayer Partner (or potential Prayer Partner),

If you are interested in praying for Pastor Bob for the next year, please plan to join us for our annual retreat, on Saturday, September 14, from 8:00 A.M. to 3:00 P.M., at the local retreat center.

Whether you can come or not, please complete the bottom of this letter, and send to the church by **Sunday, September 8.**

Sincerely,

Ken Miller
Prayer Partner Coordinator

— — — — — — — — — — — — —

Prayer Partner Retreat Sign-up

Name_____Phone_____

Address/City/State/Zip_____

_____

☐ Enclosed is $8.00 for the retreat on September 14. (Make checks payable to the church.)

☐ I cannot attend the retreat, but I'd like to continue serving as a prayer partner. (Potential prayer partners must attend the retreat in order to serve in this ministry.)

☐ I would like to discontinue serving as a prayer partner.

Please mail to: *Anytown Community Church*
555 Somewhere Lane
Anytown, USA
Attention: Church Secretary

Sample Monthly Letter
from Prayer Partner Coordinator

July 25, 1996

Dear Prayer Partner,

I want to express my gratitude to you for your contribution to the prayer partner ministry at our church. God has done incredible things as a result of our prayers. We've experienced incredible worship and ministry in our recent Sunday morning services, and Pastor Bob attributes it entirely to you and the prayer partner ministry. He tells me of the encouragement he feels as he preaches every Sunday, knowing that only a short distance away, a group of prayer partners is lifting him up in prayer.

I'm so excited about where we're going with this ministry in the coming year. I hope you'll renew your commitment to prayer partners at our upcoming retreat on September 14. (Mark your calendar!)

Enclosed is your Daily Prayer Guide for August with Pastor Bob's requests for him, his family, and our church. I've also included the Sunday Morning Prayer Schedule. Finally, I hope you are as inspired as I was by the enclosed article from Christianity Today.

Thank you again for your participation as a prayer partner. Your support of our pastor is resulting in kingdom growth at our church!

Sincerely,

Ken Miller
Prayer Partner Coordinator
Enclosures

ABOUT THE AUTHOR

John C. Maxwell is the founder of a nonprofit international Christian leadership organization called EQUIP (Encouraging Qualities Undeveloped in People). This foundation partners with individuals and organizations in the body of Christ to teach and develop leadership materials for people in the academic arena, the inner city, mission organizations, and churches worldwide.

For more than twenty-five years Maxwell was a local church senior pastor, most recently at one of America's largest churches. In 1985, he founded INJOY, an organization dedicated to helping people maximize their personal and leadership potential. Each year Maxwell speaks in person to more than 250,000 people and influences the lives of another one million through seminars, books, and tapes. He is the author of twenty-one books, including *The Success Journey, Developing the Leader Within You, Developing the Leaders Around You, Breakthrough Parenting,* and *The Winning Attitude.*

Dear Friend,

The prayer needs of pastors are so great. This year, one-third of all local church pastors will consider resigning under the weight of their responsibilities. In America, one denomination alone sees an average of four pastors resign every single day because of discouragement, personal and professional failure, and loss of purpose.

During the more **than** twenty-five years I spent in pulpit ministry, the best decision I made was to develop a prayer partner ministry. As that ministry unfolded, God led me down a fantastic road of growth. The church grew. The people grew. I grew. And exciting and effective ministries in my life were birthed. It was the most incredible experience of my pastorate.

Because I have experienced the life-changing power of a prayer partner ministry, I want to share that experience with as many churches as possible. I've made it my goal to raise up one million prayer partners for pastors in America. And that's why I've written this book and made raising up prayer partners one of EQUIP's primary purposes.

Will you be the one to make a difference in the life of your pastor and church? Are you willing to become your pastor's most valuable player? If you are ready to make one of the most strategic commitments of your life and agree to pray for your pastor for one year, then please let me know of your decision by returning the response card in this book. I would like to pray for *you* and add your name to God's expanding army of prayer partners across the nation.

Make the commitment today. It will be one of the most exciting things you ever do!

Your friend,

John Maxwell

EQUIP is a nonprofit foundation founded by John Maxwell and dedicated to raising up leaders worldwide. If we in the Christian community raise up leaders, we will gain many followers of Christ.

For more information about this unique leadership ministry, please call 1-888-993-7847

Prayer Partners
Resource List
Here are few suggested resources for starting a prayer partner ministry in your church.

Partners in Prayer book . . . . Quantity Discounts Available

The Pastor's MVP (VHS video) . . . . $ 5.00
A practical resource for recruiting prayer partners. This video consists of three parts: an introduction to the pastor, John Maxwell's inspiring MVP message, and a closing challenge encouraging viewers to become their pastor's most valuable player.

(Call for special discounts on book and video sets.)

100 Partners in Prayer Commitment Cards . . . .$ 6.00
A convenient tool for pastors to track their newly committed prayer partners. This card can also reinforce the congregation's decision to pray for their pastor.

Pastor's Prayer Partners $50.00
A complete prayer ministry resource that includes: **a VHS video** with excerpts of John Maxwell's training at a prayer partner retreat; **six audiocassettes** on prayer by John Maxwell, including two Sunday sermons challenging his congregation to a deeper commitment to prayer; **supplemental materials**, sample letters, promotional pieces, and response cards to help you develop a prayer ministry in your church.

Plus shipping and handling on all items

Call toll free 1-888-993-7847
to order prayer partner resources.

EQUIP
Encouraging Qualities Undeveloped In People

EQUIP • P.O. Box 7700 • Atlanta, GA 30357-0700 • www.prayerpartners.org